SHOP DESIGN SERIES
CAFES & RESTAURANTS
62 outstanding cafes, tearooms, cafe-bars, restaurants

目 次

第1章 複合カフェ

インディヴィ カフェ　カフェ	6
カパ 代官山店　カフェ	8
ミュゼ大阪　カフェ, ギャラリー&サロン	11
チャロン [茶虫]　ティールーム	14
フランキーボーイカフェ　カフェ	16
ティーパス　カフェ＋セレクト雑貨	18
シナモ　カフェ＋生活雑貨	20
カトル　メディアカフェ	22
クレイトンズ　カフェ＋関連商品	24
アシュビィズ オブ ロンドン 赤坂　紅茶専門店	26
銀座あけぼの　和菓子ティールーム	28
ケーキマニア　デザートカフェ	30
ヴィザヴィ 天神今泉店　ケーキカフェ	32
プルミエール　ケーキカフェ	34
ル・プティ・ブドン　パティスリーサロン・ド・テ	36
シーキューブ 芦屋店　ケーキ&カフェレストラン	38
フレスカ [三万石猪苗代店]　菓子&カフェ	40
クレーム デ ラ クレーム　シュークリーム	43
A.D.K.　イタリアンデリ&カフェ	46
ニューヨークデリ　デリ&カフェ	48
632　ベーカーリーカフェ&レストラン	50
キャスロン　ベーカリーカフェ&デザイングッズ	52
パン・ド・ケルシー　ベーカリー＋カフェレストラン	54

第2章 カフェ&ティールーム

櫻茶屋　自家焙煎珈琲店	58
ネスカフェ　カフェ	61
ロッジ　カフェ	64
珈琲クラブ　珈琲専門店	66
ミケランジェロ　オープンカフェ	68
カフェ・ド・フロール 表参道店　オープンカフェ	70
フォート マックヘンリー　エスプレッソカフェ	72
鈴木　自家焙煎珈琲店	74
ショパン　カフェ	77
ムジカ・ラ・ラ　カフェ	80
シネマカフェ　アーティスト・カフェ	82
ラ カフェ ケニア　コーヒーショップ	84
シャノアール 両国店　コーヒー専門店	86
クレシェンテ　デザートカフェ	88
ノア　カフェ&ドルチェ	90
タカノ フルーツパーラー & フルーツバー	93
ジュースプラス　ヘルスコンシャス・カフェ	96
e-ストリート ベーグルズ 虎ノ門店　ベーグルカフェ	98
レガーロ 虎ノ門店　デリカフェ	100
グリーン　ティールーム	102
嵐山 宇治庵　甘味喫茶	104
茶語　中国茶ティールーム	106
ラウンジ235　ティーラウンジ	108

第3章 カフェ レストラン

リコルディ　多目的ダイニングカフェ	112
ロータス　カフェレストラン	115
シャルボン　カフェレストラン	118
ニュートラル　カフェ・キュイジーヌ	121
クィーンズコート　キッチン&カフェ	124
ブレーク　コーヒー&グリル	126
ヴィ サ ヴィ　ダイニングカフェ	128
パリヤ 北青山　ティー・ダイニング&バー	130
グリグリア バックス カフェ　カフェ&レストラン	132
バルコニー　カフェ&レストラン	134
ちから　カフェ&レストラン	136
イズントイット お初天神店　カフェ・レストランバー	138
レゼ　カフェ	140
屯風　ダイニングカフェ	142
資生堂パーラー 横浜そごう店　レストランカフェ	144
束矢亭　ガーデンダイニング&カフェ	146

第4章 ショップデータ　149

CONTENTS

CHAPTER 1 CAFE COMPLEXES

INDIVI CAFE Cafe	6
KAPA Daikanyama Cafe	8
MUSE OSAKA Cafe, Gallery & Salon	11
CHA-LONG Tea Room	14
FRANKIE BOY CAFE Shibuya Cafe	16
TEEPASS Cafe & Goods shop	18
SINAMO Cafe & Goods shop	20
QUATRE Library Cafe	22
CRAIGHTON'S Cafe & Coffee Goods	24
ASHBYS OF LONDON Akasaka Tea House	26
GINZA AKEBONO Japanese Confectionery Bar	28
CAKE MANIA Dessert Cafe	30
VIS A VIS Tenjin-imaizumi Cake Cafe	32
PREMIER Patisserie Cafe	34
LE PETIT BEDON Patisserie-salon De Thé	36
C³ Ashiya Cake & Italian Restaurant	38
FRESCA Cafe & Confectionery	40
CREME DE LA CREME Cream Puff	43
A.D.K. Italian Deli & Cafe	46
NEW YORK DELI Deli & Cafe	48
632 Bakery Cafe & Restaurant	50
CASLON Bakery Cafe & Goods Shop	52
PAIN DE QUERCY Bakery & Cafe Restaurant	54

CHAPTER 2 CAFES & TEAROOMS

SAKURA-JAYA Coffee Shop	58
NESCAFE Cafe	61
LODGE Cafe	64
COFFEE CLUB Cafe	66
MICHELANGELO Open Cafe	68
Café de FLORE Omotesando Cafe	70
FORT McHENRY Espresso Cafe	72
SUZUKI Coffee Shop	74
CHOPIN Cafe	77
MUSICA LA LA Cafe	80
CINEMA CAFE Cafe	82
La Caffé KENYA Coffee Shop	84
CHAT NOIR Ryogoku Cafe	86
CRESCENTE Cafe	88
NOA Caffé e Dolce	90
TAKANO Fruit Parlor & Fruit Bar Fruit Parlor	93
JUICE PLUS Cafe	96
e-STREET BAGELS Toranomon Bagel Shop	98
REGARO Toranomon Deli-cafe	100
GREEN Tearoom	102
Arashiyama UJIAN Japanese Cafe	104
CHA YŪ Chinese Tearoom	106
LOUNGE 235 Tearoom	108

CHAPTER 3 CAFE-RESTAURANTS

RICORDI Dining-cafe	112
LOTUS Cafe-restaurant	115
CHARBON Cafe-restaurant	118
NEUT Cafe-Cuisine	121
QUEEN'S COURT Kitchen & Cafe	124
BREAK Coffee & Grill	126
VIS-A-VIS Dining & Cafe	128
PARIYA Kita-aoyama Tea, Dining & Bar	130
GRIGRIA BACS CAFE Cafe & Restaurant	132
BALCONY Cafe & Restaurant	134
CHIKARA Cafe & Restaurant	136
ISN'T IT? Ohatsu-tenjin Cafe, Restaurant-bar	138
LAISSER Cafe	140
TON-FU Dining & Cafe	142
SHISEIDO Parlour Yokohama-sogo Restaurant Cafe	144
TABAYATEI Garden Dining & Cafe	146

CHAPTER 4 SHOPS DATAS

	149

ABBREVIATIONS 略号ほか

A/C	Air Conditioner エアコン, 空調機		CB	Concrete Block コンクリートブロック
Cr	Cloakroom クローク		CL	Clear Lacquer finish クリアラッカー仕上げ
Ctr	Counter カウンター		EP	Emulsion Paint finish エマルションペイント仕上げ
DF	Drinking Fountain ドリンクスペンサー		FRP	Fiber-glass Reinforced Plastics ガラス繊維強化プラスチック
DS	Duct Space ダクトスペース		FB	Flat Bar フラットバー
DT	Display Table ディスプレイテーブル		Fix	Fixed fitting はめごろし
DW	Dumb Waiter, Lift ダムウエーター, リフト		FL	Fluorescent Lamp 蛍光灯
EH	Entrance Hall 入り口ホール, エントランスホール		H	Height 高さ
Elec	Electrical Room 電気室		HL	Hair-Line finish ヘアライン仕上げ
Elv	Elevator エレベーター		JB	Jet Burner finish ジェットバーナー仕上げ
Esc	Escalator エスカレーター		JP	Jet Polish finish ジェットポリッシュ仕上げ
FR	Fitting Room フィッティングルーム		OF	Oil Finish オイル仕上げ
F·Rf	Freezer & Refrigerator 冷凍冷蔵庫		OP	Oil Paint finish オイルペイント仕上げ
GL	Ground Level グランドレベル, 基準地盤面		OS	Oil Stain finish オイルステイン仕上げ
Hg	Hanger ハンガー, ハンガー棚		OSB	Oriented Strand Board 構造用合板, エンジニアードウッド
KR	Kettle Room 湯沸かし室		OSCL	Oil Stain Clear Lacquer finish オイルステイン・クリアラッカー仕上げ
LR	Locker Room ロッカールーム		PB	Plaster Board, Gypsum Board 石こうボード
Mir	Mirror ミラー, 鏡		PC	Precast Concrete プレキャストコンクリート
Mech	Mechanical Room 機械室		Pl	Plate プレート, 平板
MWC	Men's Water Closet 男性用トイレ		PvC	Polyvinyl Chloride ポリ塩化ビニル
Pn	Pantry パントリー		RC	Reinforced Concrete 鉄筋コンクリート
PS	Pipe Shaft パイプシャフト		S	Steel frame 鉄骨
PR	Powder Room 化粧室		SRC	Steel framed Reinforced Concrete 鉄骨鉄筋コンクリート
PT	Package Table 包装台		SUS	Stainless Steel ステンレススチール
R	Register, Cashier レジ, キャッシャー		t	thickness 厚み
RD	Reception Desk 受付, フロント		UC	Urethane Clear finish ウレタンクリア仕上げ
Rsv	Reservoir 受水槽		VP	Vinyl Paint finish ビニルペイント仕上げ
Rf	Refrigerator 冷蔵庫		w	width 幅
Sc	Showcase ショーケース		@	pitch ピッチ, 間隔
Sh	Shelf 棚, 商品展示棚		φ	diameter 直径
SpC	Sample Case サンプルケース, 見本棚			
SR	Staff Room スタッフルーム			
SS	Service Station サービスステーション			
St	Stage ステージ, ディスプレイステージ			
SW	Show Window ショーウインドー			
VM	Vending Machine 自動販売機			
WA	Waiting Area 待合スペース, 客待ちスペース			
WbR	Windbreak Room 風除室			
Wh	Warehouse 倉庫			
WT	Working Table 作業テーブル			
WWC	Women's Water Closet 女性用トイレ, 化粧室			
AEP	Acryl Emulsion Paint finish アクリルエマルションペイント仕上げ			
ALC	Autoclaved Light-weight Concrete 軽量気泡コンクリート			

本書は1995年から2001年までの月刊商店建築(増刊号を含む)に掲載された作品をセレクトし、構成されたものです。作品に関するコメントは、雑誌に掲載された設計者とクライアントサイドのコメントをもとに編集者がまとめています。なお、巻末の施設データのうち、営業的なデータは雑誌掲載時のものなので、変更されている場合があります。

This book collects projects selected from monthly magazine Shotenkenchiku back numbers (including extra issues) published from 1995 through 2001. All the texts except some of the new projects are summaries by the editor of comments by the designers and clients.

SHOP DESIGN SERIES
CHAPTER 1

CAFE COMPLEXES

ファッションブランド店へのプロローグ

インディヴィ カフェ

東京・新宿

Cafe **INDIVI CAFE**

Shinjuku, Tokyo
Designer: Masamichi Katayama
Photographer: Shinichi Sato

設計：エイチ・デザイン アソシエイツ
施工：ディーブレーン

1

2

3

1. デパートのパブリック通路に面したファサード
2. 外部道路からデパートの入り口ガラス越しに見たファサード
3. 店内からファサードを通して外部道路方向を見る
4. 壁面にミラーを配した客席全景をレジ側から見る

1. A view of the facade facing the public passage
2. A view from the outside street to the facade
3. A view from the seating to the outside street
4. A whole view of the seating from the cashier side

伝統的なボキャブラリーを再構築

ファッションブティックが、ブランドイメージにふさわしいデザインのカフェを併設するようになったのは、最近の傾向である。そのきっかけをつくったともいえる「インディヴィ」が、東京・新宿のデパート内に設けたのがこのカフェ。デパートの入り口に面した場所に配されたカフェの奥には、「インディヴィ」など同じ系列のブティックが3店舗並んでいる。
このカフェのデザインの特徴は、デパートの店内にもかかわらず、道路に面したオープンカフェのテラス席のようにサッシのファサードを持っていることである。これは、オーソドックスでクラシカルなカフェのイメージをあえて取り込み、再構築するためである。また、同様の理由で内部壁面にミラーが取り入れられており、壁に向いた客は退屈することなく、店内の人の動きを楽しむことができる。

Indivi Cafe

Fashion boutiques establishing cafes with designs matching their brand image is a recent phenomenon. Indivi, which set this trend, created this cafe in a department store in Shinjuku, Tokyo.
There are three Indivi-affiliated boutiques in the back of the cafe, which faces the department store entrance. Despite being located in a department store, Indivi Cafe features a sash facade like those found in open cafes that have terrace seating facing the street. This bold move is intended to incorporate and reconstruct the orthodox, classical image of a cafe. And for similar reasons, the walls inside the cafe are adorned with mirrors, permitting customers to watch the movement of people.

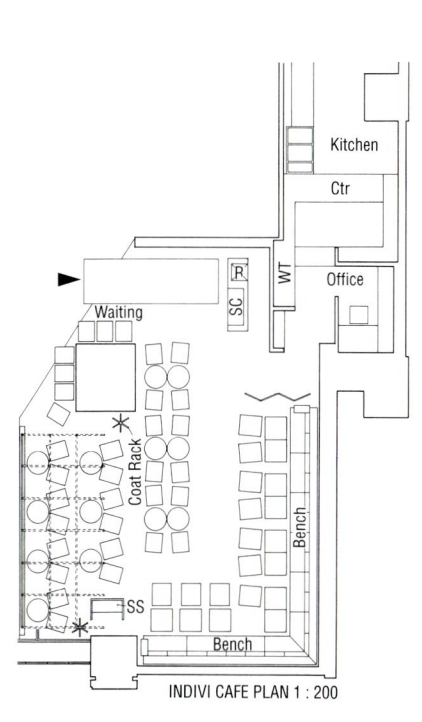

INDIVI CAFE PLAN 1 : 200

ファッションブランドビル地下のカフェ | Cafe **KAPA Daikanyama**

カパ 代官山
東京・恵比寿

Ebisu-nishi, Tokyo
Designer: Masamichi Katayama
Photographer: Shinichi Sato

設計：エイチ・デザイン
　　　アソシエイツ
施工：ディーブレーン

1

抜けた明るさの"場"をデザイン

代官山は，若者の街・渋谷に隣接しているにもかかわらず，高級住宅地域にファッショナブルなブティックが点在するハイセンスなエリアであり，古い集合住宅の再開発によって新しい商業ビルができたこともあって，界隈を訪れる人も増えている。代官山駅前に位置していた元アクセサリーブランドのフラッグシップショップを改装したこの地下1階，地上2階建てのファッションビルは，同じ系列のブティックが3店舗とカフェで構成されている。
カフェは地下1階の奥に配されているので自然光がまったく入らないが，インテリアデザインは条件を逆手に取り，まるで外部でコーヒーを楽しんでいるかのような明るさに満ちた空間が提案された。天井すべてと壁の一面は，表面を覆っている乳白色のアクリル板の裏側に埋め込まれた蛍光灯により発光体と化し，内部空間を照らし出している。

Kapa Daikanyama

Though it is adjacent to Shibuya, a town for young people, Daikanyama is a high-class residential area dotted with fashionable boutiques. Old apartment buildings have been redeveloped into new commercial buildings, helping to bring more visitors to the neighborhood. This three-story building in front of Daikanyama Station contains three affiliated fashion boutiques and a cafe. The remodeled building was formerly the flagship shop of a fashion accessory brand.
The cafe is located in the first underground floor, and therefore receives no natural light. But refusing to be limited by their environment, the interior designers have created a space so bright it almost gives customers the impression they are drinking coffee outdoors. Fluorescent lights placed behind the milky white acrylic panels covering the ceiling and one wall transform them into luminous bodies that brighten the interior.

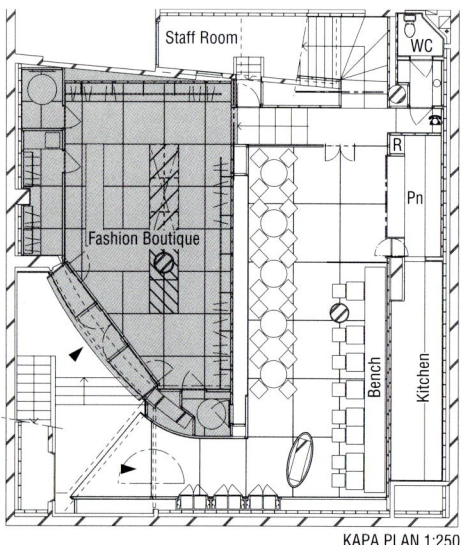

KAPA PLAN 1:250

1. パントリー側からガラスのパーティション越しに見たベンチ席
2. 店内奥から入り口側を見た客席全景
3. 地下1階通路から見た入り口まわり
4. 入り口アプローチから店内を見る
5. パントリー側から見た光り壁と光り天井

1. A view of the bench seating from the pantry side
2. A whole view of the seating from the inner part
3. A view of the entrance on the first basement floor
4. A view from the entrance to the inside
5. A view of the lighting wall and ceiling from the pantry side

アートギャラリーと一体化したカフェ＆サロン

ミュゼ大阪
大阪・南堀江

Cafe, Gallery, Salon **MUSE OSAKA**

Minami-horie, Osaka
Designer: Yoshihiko Mamiya
Photographer: Seiryo Yamada

設 計：インフィクス
施 工：まこと建設

1

2

3

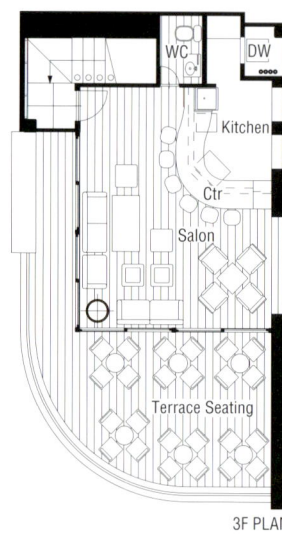
3F PLAN

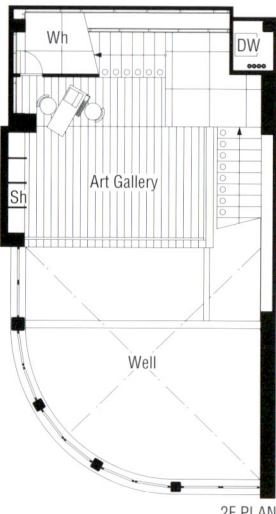
2F PLAN

1. 吹き抜けに面した2階アートギャラリー
2. 南側から見た正面ファサード夜景
3. 2階から吹き抜けを通して下の1階カフェ客席を見る
4. 1階カフェの入り口側から2階への階段方向を見る
5. 1階カフェ入り口右側から見た客席全景

1. A view of the art gallery on the second floor
2. A night view of the facade from the south
3. A down view from the second floor to the first floor a cafe
4. A view from the entrance side to the stairs on the first floor a cafe
5. A view of the first floor a cafe from the stairs side

建物全体をミュージアムに見立てる

大阪の代表的な繁華街・ミナミに隣接してできた通称・アメリカ村は、近年、関西ヤング文化の情報発信基地として若者が集まる地域である。アメリカ村の発展に大きな力を発揮したプロデューサー的な存在であるオーナーが、新しい構想の下にアメリカ村の西の外れに完成させたのが、この施設である。
フランス語でミュージアムを意味するミュゼという名前の通り、アートギャラリーを中心とした複合施設で、1階がカフェ、2階がギャラリー、3階がサロンという構成。アートを鑑賞した後は、ゆったりした気分でコーヒーを飲み、サロンで知人たちと情報交換をしてもらおうというオーナーの意図通り、新しい刺激と文化を求めてさまざまな人々がここを訪れている。

Muse Osaka

Recent years have seen the area popularly known as America-mura, located adjacent to the representative Osaka shopping area of Minami, become the information center of the Kansai region's youth culture and a gathering place for young people. The owner of the Muse has adroitly contributed to the area's development, acting as a sort of producer. She built Muse on the western outskirts of America-mura based on a novel concept. Faithful to the meaning of the French word muse (museum), this complex centers on an art gallery. The first floor houses a cafe, the second floor a gallery and the third floor a salon. Just as the owner planned, Salon Muse attracts a variety of visitors who come in search of stimulation and culture. They take an appreciative look at the art and then enjoy a relaxing cup of coffee while exchanging opinions with their friends.

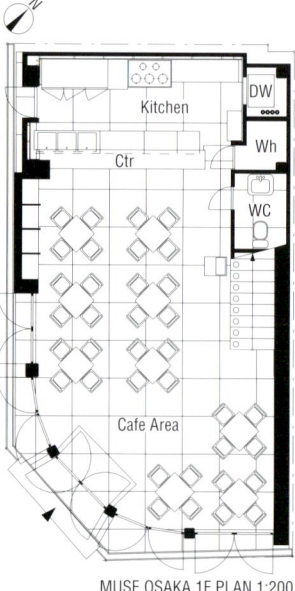
MUSE OSAKA 1F PLAN 1:200

ファッションビルの通路を利用したティールーム | Tea Room **CHA-LONG**

チャロン [茶虫]

大阪・南船場

Bakuro-machi, Osaka
Designer: Yoshihiko Mamiya
Photographer: Seiryo Yamada

設 計：インフィクス
施 工：キクスイ

1

2

3

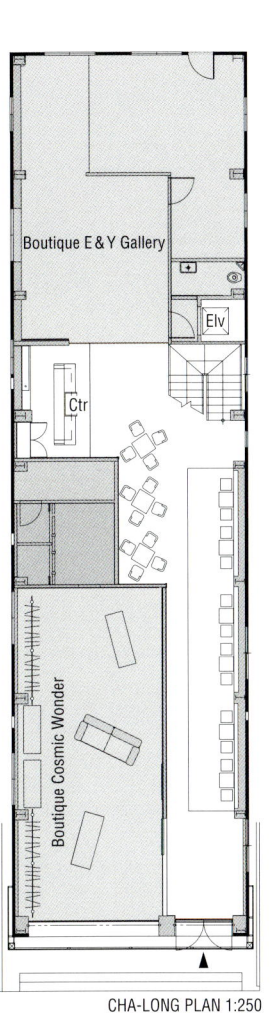

CHA-LONG PLAN 1:250

1. 道路から見たビル全体のファサード。
   カフェは入り口右側通路に沿って奥へ続く
2. 2階の階段下り口から見た2階ブティックと
   1階カフェ
3. 1階奥の階段わきから入り口方向へ
   カフェ客席を見る
4. 1階のビル通路を利用したカフェ客席は
   アートギャラリー的な雰囲気

1. A night view of the building from the street
2. A view from the stairs to the second floor a bouitique and the first floor a cafe
3. A view of the first floor a cafe from the stairs side
4. A view of the first floor a cafe under the skylight

トップライトによるギャラリー的空間

大阪・南船場は繊維関係を扱う問屋街であったが、隣接する繁華街・心斎橋とを隔てていた幹線道路の下層に地下街ができたことにより人の流れが変わり、ファッショナブルなブティックが次々とオープンするなど、新しい商業立地として注目を集めている。ティールーム・チャロンは、以前は倉庫であった南船場の4階建てファッションビルの1階に位置する。

ビルへの入り口通路や2階への階段まわりなど、パブリックな空間を巧みに利用したこのティールームは、ビル内の四つのブティックを連結する機能を持つとともに、買い物客にしばしの休息時間を提供する役割を果たしている。入り口から続く通路に沿って設けられた客席部分には、トップライトから自然光が降り注ぎ、また、2階まで続く高く白い壁面には巨大な絵画が飾られ、アートギャラリーとして来客の目を楽しませている

Cha-long

Minami-senba, Osaka, was an area of textile wholesalers, but its pedestrian traffic changed when an underground shopping mall was built under a main thoroughfare beyond the adjacent shopping area of Shinsaibashi. Minami-senba is now drawing new notice as a commercial location after a series of fashionable boutiques opened there. Tearoom Cha-Long is located there on the first floor of a former warehouse that now primarily contains fashion shops. This tearoom makes clever use of public spaces, including the hallway in front of the entrance and a stairwell to the second floor. Cha-Long serves two functions: to link the building's four boutiques and to give shoppers a place to rest. Natural light pours through a skylight into the seating area built along the hallway from the entrance. The white walls that stretch up to the second floor are adorned with enormous artwork, giving visitors a gallery to occupy their eyes.

ブランドのコンセプトを体現したカフェ

Cafe **FRANKIE BOY CAFE Shibuya**

フランキーボーイカフェ
東京・渋谷

Udagawa-cho, Tokyo
Designer: Keiichi Ooki
Photographer: Hiro Photo

設 計：ア・ファクトリー
施 工：ア・ファクトリー

1 
2

1. 渋谷のパルコ本店前に位置するビル全体のファサード。3階がカフェ
2. 道路側に面した屋外のテラス席
3. レジから店内奥方向を見る
4. 店内中央のガラスで覆われた四角錐の吹き抜け

1. A view of the building facade from the street
2. A view of the outdoor terrace seating
3. A whole view of the cafe seating from the cashier side
4. A view of the center well covered with a glass canopy

3

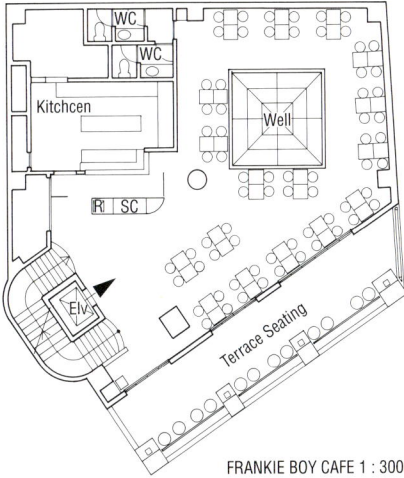

FRANKIE BOY CAFE 1 : 300

アメリカの良き時代がテーマ

若者の街、東京・渋谷にあるファッションブティック・イーストボーイの本店ビル3階にこのカフェはある。地下1階から2階までを占めるイーストボーイは「This is America」をコンセプトに、若い女性を対象としたファッション雑貨やウエアを販売している。

カフェのインテリアは、イーストボーイのコンセプトと一体化されており、'50～'60年代のアメリカをイメージさせるジュークボックス、シーリングファン、ネオンの壁時計などが配され、全体的に明るいアメリカン調でまとめられている。また、店内中央に設けられた大きなガラス張りの吹き抜けから、下部の2階ブティック売り場が垣間見え、来客はどの階にいてもビル全体の統一されたテイストが感じられるようになっている。

Frankie Boy Cafe

This cafe is on the third floor of the head office building of fashion boutique East Boy in Tokyo's Shibuya ward, a district for young people. East Boy, which fills the space from the first underground story to the second story, is based on the concept "This is America", and sells fashion accessories and clothing to young women.

The cafe interior is based on the same concept. It is decorated with items that recall the America of the " '50s and '60s a jukebox, ceiling fan and neon wall clock" to set an overall warm, American tone. A glass-covered well in the center of the cafe provides a glimpse of the boutique's second-story sales floor below, and the building is set up so that customers experience an identical sense of taste on every floor.

テラスのあるカフェ＋セレクト雑貨店

Cafe & Goods TEEPASS

ティーパス
神奈川・茅ヶ崎市

Chigasaki, Kanagawa
Designer: Yuichi Oda
Photographer: Keisuke Miyamoto

設 計：アート・スタジオ　ザ・ディープ
施 工：アミナ住研

2

1　3

サーフィンのイメージを具現化

東京に近い海浜リゾート地であり、高級住宅地としても発展してきた湘南地方。そのほぼ中央にある茅ヶ崎市の海岸近くにティーパスは位置する。道路に面した前面中央に雑貨売り場である八角形のタワーを持ち、その両側をカフェ部分が取り囲む。両側の屋根が飛行機の尾翼のような形状をしているのは、下部のオープンデッキと入り口まわりに風の通り道をつくると同時に、サーフィンのメッカである茅ヶ崎のイメージを表現したもの。もともとこの敷地は資材置き場として使われていた場所で、オーナーのバレーボール仲間が気軽に集まって楽しめるスペースをつくるためにショップが企画された。内部はカントリーなイメージを出すため、米松などの木材が使われており、それに白のタイルが組み合わされている。

Teepass

The Shonan district is a seaside resort near Tokyo that has begun to develop into a high-class residential area. Cafe and goods market Teepas is located near the coast in the central Shonan city of Chigasaki. It consists of a general market in a road-front octagonal tower that is flanked on both sides by a cafe. The airplane-tail-shaped roofs on each side serve a dual purpose: to direct the wind onto the open deck and entrance area below, and to express the surfing Mecca image of Chigasaki. The lot on which Teepas stands was originally used to store materials. The owner built the shop on a whim as a place to enjoy her volleyball friends. To convey the image of the countryside, American pine and white tile were used for the interior.

1. 東面右端の入り口まわり外観。左側に見えるのはショップタワー
2. 板貼りの屋外テラス席から内部客席を見る
3. ショップコーナーから見たカフェ厨房とベンチ客席
4. 店内中央から奥のベンチ客席と屋外テラス客席を見る
5. 入り口左側に配された八角形の雑貨ショップタワー

1. A view of the entrance from the east street
2. A view from the outdoor terrace to the bench seating
3. A view of the kitchen and bench seating from the shop area
4. A view of the bench seating and outdoor terrace from the center
5. A view of the shop area facing the east street

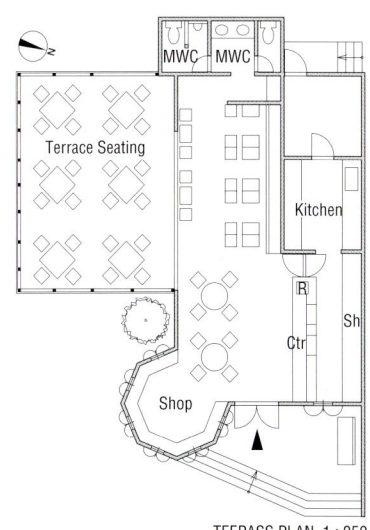

TEEPASS PLAN 1:250

雑貨店に見えない生活雑貨とカフェの店

シナモ
京都・寺町通

Cafe & Goods **SINAMO**

Teramachi-doori, Kyoto
Designer: Yasumichi Morita
Photographer: Seiryo Yamada

設 計：森田恭道デザイン事務所
施 工：スペースデザイン アスク

1. 入り口から奥へと続く細長い店内。右側壁面はミラーに映り込んだ虚像
2. 店内最奥部分に配された杉材ムクのバーカウンター

1. A view of the long and slender interior from the entrance
2. A view of the bar counter on the inner part

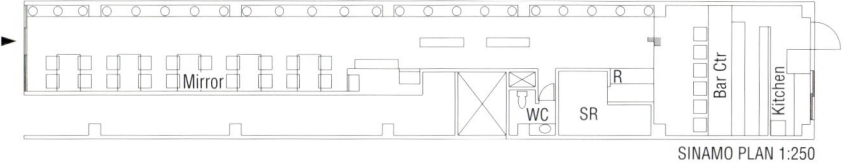

SINAMO PLAN 1:250

テーブルスタンドの林立する空間

奈良とともに日本を代表する古都・京都の寺町通り二条は、全国に知られた伝統ある骨董屋やギャラリーが多くあり、観光客がしばしば訪れる場所である。ここに新しくできたシナモは、以前は別の場所で生活スタイルを提案する雑貨の専門店を経営していたが、移転を機に雑貨とカフェ、バーを一体化した店舗となった。

客席片側の棚に数多くのテーブルスタンド照明をディスプレイし、反対側のミラー貼りの壁面に映し出された店内は、一見、雑貨屋に見えないユニークさである。オープン後の来客は70％が女性客で、また、売り上げの比率は飲食と雑貨では約7：3となっており、飲食のウエートのほうが高い。今後は、雑貨の売上比率を高くするのが課題とのことである。

Sinamo

On the street known as Teramachi-Doori Ni-Jo in Kyoto, the former capital that together with Nara symbolizes Japan, there are many nationally known, traditional antique shops and galleries that draw tourists to the area. Sinamo was a lifestyle products specialty shop before recently relocating here and becoming a combined general store, cafe and bar. The interior, where numerous table lamps are displayed on shelves on one side of the customer seating, immediately conveys a uniqueness that conceals Sinamo's identity as a general store. Seventy percent of Sinamo's customers are women, and its ratio of cafe and bar sales to general store sales is about 7 to 3. The managers are working to increase the sales of their general merchandise.

四つのテーマを提供するメディアカフェ

カトル
名古屋・名駅

Library Cafe **QUATRE**

Meieki, Nagoya
Designer: Ryu Kosaka
Photographer: Nacása & Partners

設 計：乃村工芸社
施 工：乃村工芸社

1

2

3

アナログツールによる落ち着いた空間

JR名古屋駅の上にそびえるJRセントラルタワーズは、ギネスブックでも認定された世界最大のステーションビルである。その12階、13階を占めるタワーズプラザの一角に、カトルはオープンした。会員制のメンバーが利用するこのライブラリーカフェは、雑誌、DVD、インターネット、CSTVの四つのメディアを使って、アート、食、旅行、花という四つの分野の情報を利用できるという新しいタイプのメディアカフェである。
情報検索で時間を過ごした後は、カフェ&バーでゆったりとくつろぐという「個人」の楽しみを提供する場であり、平日の昼間は若い女性、夜間はビジネスマン、キャリアウーマンの利用が多い。カフェのまわりにパソコンやDVDを配した暗めの店内構成は、照明効果と相まって、落ち着ける空間として好評である。

Quatre

JR Central Towers, which stand above the Japan Rail Nagoya Station, are recognized in the Guinness Book of Records as the largest train station building in the world. Quatre opened in one corner of Towers Plaza, which occupies the 12th and 13th floors. It is a new type of media cafe where members can obtain information on art, food, travel and flowers from magazines, DVDs, the Internet and the CSTV subscription cable channel. Quatre is intended to give customers a place to relax and enjoy individual pursuits after they find the information they need. It is patronized mainly by young women on weekdays during the day and by business-people at night. The subdued lighting and configuration of the interior, where personal computers and DVD stations have been placed on the perimeter of the cafe, are said to help people relax.

4

5

1. 本がディスプレイされた中央の柱まわり棚
2. 入り口まわり外観
3. 窓側開口部に面した右奥の客席
4. 入り口右側のバックライトに浮き上がる本棚
5. 右奥客席から中央の柱まわり棚方向を見る
6. 店内最奥のカウンター席

1. A view of the shelves surrounding the center pillar
2. A view of the entrance from the outside
3. A view of the lounge facing the window
4. A view of the book shelves with back lighting
5. A view from the lounge to the center pillar
6. A view of the counter seating on the inner part

6

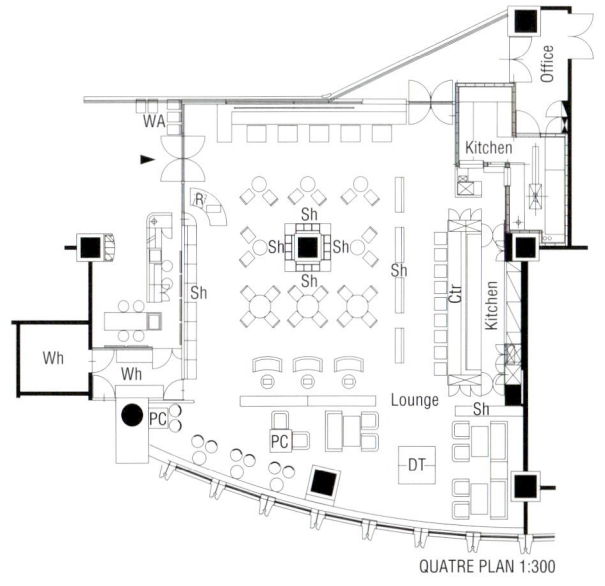

QUATRE PLAN 1:300

焙煎メーカーによるカフェ＋関連商品の店 | Cafe & Coffee Goods **CRAIGHTON'S**

クレイトンズ
東京・六本木

Roppongi, Tokyo
Designer: Shigeru Uchida
Photographer: Satoshi Asakawa

設 計：内田 繁＋スタジオ80
施 工：スペース

1

2

3

吹き抜け空間を彩る光サイフォン

大手のコーヒー焙煎，小売り企業が，東京・六本木に出店したデモンストレーションを兼ねたフラッグシップショップ。1階がコーヒー豆や関連グッズの販売スペースと独自に開発した光サイフォンによるコーヒーをテイクアウトできるセルフサービスのカフェ，2階がフルサービスのカフェである。また，2階の一角には透明なガラスのディバイダーで仕切られたプライベートルームが設けられている。インテリアの特徴は1階と2階をつなぐ高さ6mの吹き抜けで，1階の色鮮やかなブルーのカウンター上には光サイフォンが並んでいる。また，この吹き抜け空間の天井と壁はブラウン色の南洋材のパネルで覆われ，ハイグレードな雰囲気を醸し出している。

Craighton's

A major coffee roaster opened the retail store Craighton's in Roppongi, Tokyo, as a flagship shop and a place to demonstrate its products. The first floor serves as a sales space for coffee beans and related goods, and as a cafe where customers use an original type of optical siphon to serve themselves takeout coffee. The second floor is a full-service cafe, one corner of which is partitioned off using a transparent, glass divider to create a private room. The interior of Craighton's is distinguished by a 6-meter well connecting the first and second floors and by the first floor's brilliant blue counter on which optical siphons stand in a row. This ceiling and walls of the well are covered in brown, tropical-wood paneling, creating a high-grade ambiance.

1. 1階入り口から見た店内。右側がセルフサービスの光サイフォンを使ったカウンター
2. 1階の階段上り口から見たセルフサービスカウンター
3. 1階奥のレジわきからコーヒー関連ショップエリアを見る
4. ガラスで仕切られた2階のクレイトンズルーム
5. 2階のクレイトンズルームから見たフルサービス用カウンター

1. A view from the entrance on the first floor
2. A view of the optical siphon counter on the first floor
3. A view from the cashier side to the coffee beans shop on the first floor
4. A view of the Craighton's room on the second floor
5. A view of the optical siphon counter on the second floor

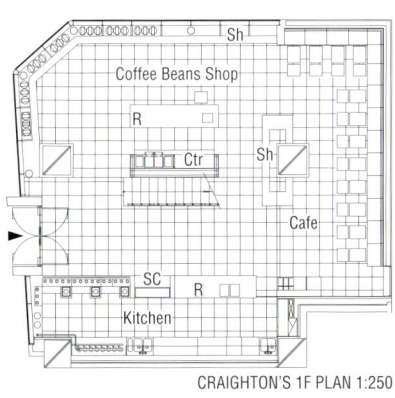

CRAIGHTON'S 1F PLAN 1:250

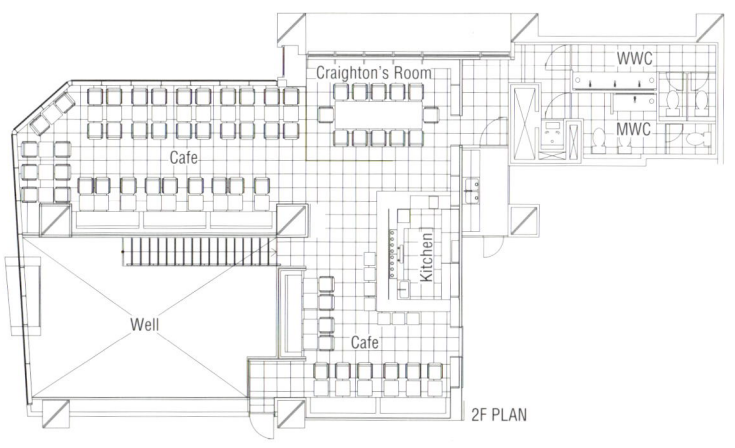

2F PLAN

セルフサービスによる本格的紅茶店

アシュビィズ オブ ロンドン 赤坂

東京・赤坂

Tea House **ASHBYS OF LONDON Akasaka**

Akasaka, Tokyo
Designer: CIA
Photographer: Kaku Ootaki

設 計：CIA
施 工：松美舎

1

英国スタイルのテラス風インテリア

東京・赤坂にできたこのティーハウスは女性をメーンターゲットに、コーヒーのように気軽に飲める紅茶の専門店を目指して企画された。出店に当たっては、英国で実績のあるアシュビィズがブランドとして選定され、30種類の本格的な紅茶が1杯280円の低価格から楽しめ、スコーンやケーキ、サンドイッチも用意されている。
テラス風のインテリアは、壁面が英国調のナチュラルカラーのウッドパネルで、本棚の上部にはさまざまなティーカップがディスプレイされ、その下部には紅茶の歴史を感じさせる絵画が飾られるなど、本場・英国紅茶を楽しむにふさわしい環境が用意された。意図したとおり、20～30歳代の若いOLで店内はにぎわい、一日中、華やかな雰囲気に包まれている。

Ashbys of London

The casual teahouse Ashbys of London in Akasaka, Tokyo, mainly targets women. Ashbys tea was chosen because it has a track record in England, and there are 30 varieties available at the low price of 280 yen per cup. Scones, cakes, sandwiches and the like round out the menu. The walls of the terracelike interior are covered with English-style natural-color wood paneling. Various teacups and pictures that convey the history of tea are displayed on bookshelves. These elements combine to create an environment appropriate for enjoying authentic English tea. As intended, the shop is filled throughout the day with female office workers in their 20s and 30s, who help create a bustling, merry atmosphere.

1. 背後の開口部窓から見た奥の客席
2. 道路から見たファサード
3. 入り口右側の関連グッズコーナー
4. 店内中央のキッチンカウンター

1. A view of the inner part seating through the window
2. A view of the facade from the street
3. A view of the tea goods shop area
4. A view of the counter on the center

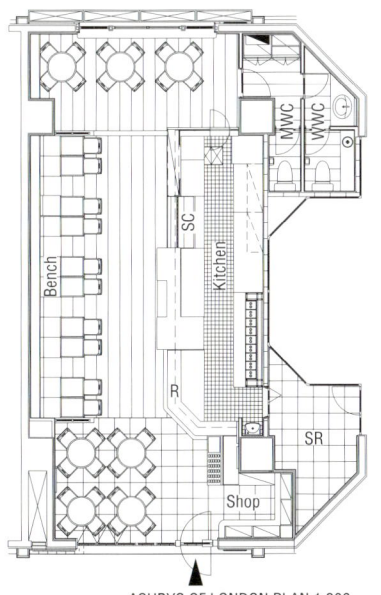

ASHBYS OF LONDON PLAN 1:200

老舗煎餅屋のティールーム兼応接スペース

銀座あけぼの

東京・銀座

Japanese Confectionery Bar **GINZA AKEBONO**

Ginza, Tokyo
Designer: Kunikazu Takatori
Photographer: Yoshio Shiratori

設 計：高取空間計画
施 工：イシマル

新しい時代の古き良きテイストを目指す

日本を代表する歴史を持つ繁華街・銀座も海外ブランドの出店ラッシュや新しい業態の進出により、かつての伝統的な魅力が薄れつつある。煎餅の老舗である「あけぼの」が新しい時代にふさわしい、古き良き時代のテイストを感じさせる場をつくろうという意図でこの和菓子バーは誕生した。従来は倉庫として使われていた地下を、来客の応接スペースとして使うとともに、和菓子バーとしてお茶と一緒に楽しんでもらおうという企画である。店内の中央を占める南洋材ムクのカウンター上には、オリジナルに開発された黒や朱の器が置かれ、片肘付きの木のイスも新たにデザインされた。にぎやかな表通りに面した1階とは隔絶された静寂の空間が好評で、常連客を含めて1日約50人前後の客が訪れている。

Ginza Akebono

New business conditions and a rush to open new stores have caused the traditional appeal of even the historic business district of Ginza, which to many symbolizes Japan, to continue to decline. The managers of the longstanding senbei (rice cracker) shop Akebono created the wagashi (Japanese confectionery) bar Ginza Akebono to offer traditional goodies in a way that appeals to a new era. The shop serves its Japanese sweets along with tea in an underground space that was formerly used for storage. In the center of the shop, original black and red containers rest on a solid-tropical-wood counter, next to which are wooden armchairs, also an original design. This quiet space sequestered from the bustling street in front of the first floor enjoys a good reputation, attracting about 50 customers a day, including regular customers.

1. 通りから見た1階煎餅店のファサード。店内左側に地下への階段が見える
2. エントランスホールのレジカウンター
3. 店内奥から見たカウンター席。片肘付きのイスはオリジナルデザイン
4. カウンター内部から背後のベンチ席方向を見る。器も新しく開発されたもの
5. 入り口側から見たカウンター席全景。暗めの照明による落ち着いた雰囲気

1. A view of the senbei shop facade from the street on the first floor
2. A view of the entrance hall and cashier counter on the first basement floor
3. A view of the counter seating from the inner part on the first basement floor
4. A view from the counter to the bench on the first basement floor
5. A whole view of the counter from the entrance side on the first basement floor

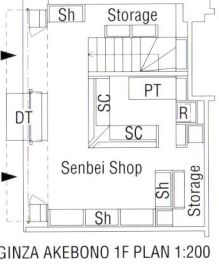

GINZA AKEBONO 1F PLAN 1:200

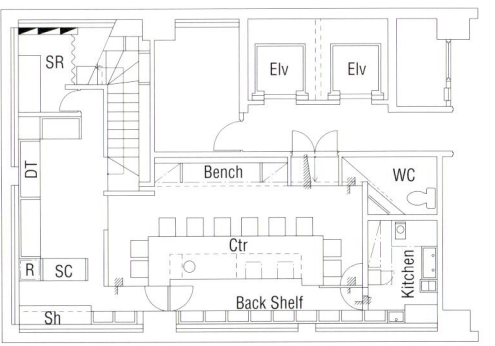

B1F PLAN

アンテナショップとしてのデザートカフェ

ケーキマニア
横浜・新港町

Dessert Cafe CAKE MANIA

Shinko-cho, Yokohama
Designer: Takashi Miyazato
Photographer: Kaku Ootaki

設 計：乃村工芸社
施 工：乃村工芸社

1. 外部に面したファサード
2. ビル内部側入り口から見たケーキ売り場と客席
3. 客席A内部から客席B方向を見る
4. 客席Bからグリッド壁面に囲まれた客席Aを見る

1. A view of the facade facing the outdoor
2. A view of the cake shop area from the building passage side entrance
3. A view from the seating A to the seating B
4. A view of the seating A surrounded with the grid walls

カラフルなケーキを引き立てる純白空間

外国との貿易摩擦を解消するという目的でつくられた横浜ワールドポーターズ。そのビルの1階にケーキマニアはつくられた。病院の食堂やテーマパークのために冷凍ケーキを製造している企業の経営で、ダイレクトに顧客の声を聞き、商品開発をするためのアンテナショップという位置付けである。4.5mの高い天井を持つ店内は、カラフルな家具で遊び心を表現したいというクライアントの要望と色とりどりのケーキたちを引き立たせるために、真っ白なキャンバスのような空間がコンセプトとされた。長さ7mのステンレス製ケーキケース、ラウンドした下がり壁、2枚のグリッド壁、天井まで延びる巨大なアートフレームという、違う表情と役割を持つ四つのエレメントが、この空間をダイナミックでキュートなものにしている。

Cake Mania

The shopping mall Yokohama World Porters was built to alleviate friction with other countries over Japan's trade surplus. Cake Mania is located on its first floor. Managed by a company that produces frozen cake for hospital cafeterias and theme parks, the shop serves as an antenna that lets the company listen directly to customers to aid in its product development. The interior, which has a 4.5 meter high ceiling, was made completely white like a canvas to add to the visual appeal of the multicolored cakes. Colorful furniture appeals to customers sense of play. Four elements disparate in appearance and function - a seven meter stainless steel cake case; a round down wall; two grid walls; and an enormous art frame stretching to the ceiling combine to make this space dynamic and cute.

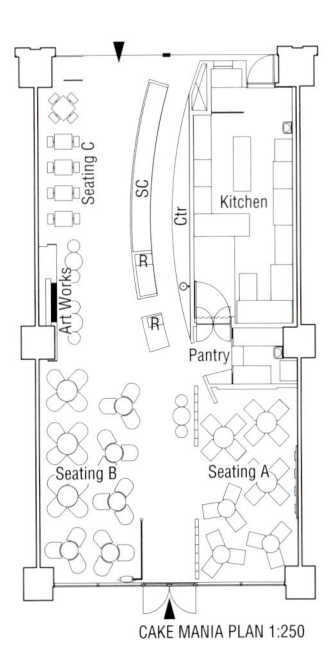

CAKE MANIA PLAN 1:250

イートインを重視したケーキカフェ

Cake Cafe **VIS A VIS Tenjin-imaizumi**

ヴィザヴィ 天神今泉店

福岡・今泉

Imaizumi, Fukuoka
Designer: Toshinori Kamiya
Photographer: Toshihisa Ishii

設計：神谷デザイン事務所
施工：占部製作所

左右の壁面デザインで店内を左右に分割

福岡市の中心繁華街・天神に近い場所に、このケーキカフェはオープンした。郊外型のケーキショップ、カフェレストランを何店舗か経営している企業が、初めて出店する都市型の店舗である。既存のケーキショップはイートインよりテイクアウトの機能を重視したつくりであったが、この店の場合は、バスストップの前という好立地からイートインにも力が注がれた。
道路に面した前面がガラス張りの内部は、中央のケーキケースを挟んで右側壁面が白いタイル貼り、左側壁面が古木材という対照的な素材で構成されている。これはケーキがディスプレイされている右側はクリーンで女性的なイメージ、客席のある左側はゆったりとイートインできる温かで親しみやすい雰囲気を創出するためである。

Vis á Vis

The cake cafe Vis á Vis is located near the central Fukuoka business district of Tenjin. It is the first urban establishment opened by a company managing several suburban cake shops and cafe and restaurants. The company's other shops emphasize takeout, but because Vis á Vis is favorably located in front of a bus stop, it puts energy into its eat-in business also. The front of Vis á Vis faces the road and is constructed of glass windows. Inside, the central cake case is placed between two walls of contrasting material: white tile on the right and aged wood on the left. The intention is to create a clean, feminine image on the right side, where the cakes are displayed, and a leisurely, warm and fun atmosphere on the left, where customers eat.

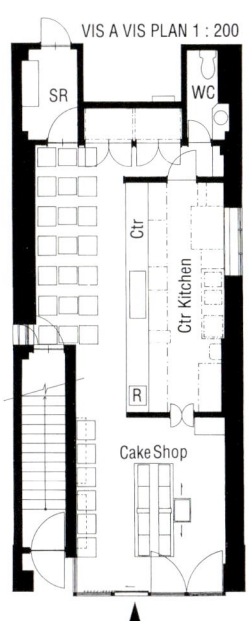

1. 道路から見たファサード夜景。左右壁面に対照的な素材を使用
2. 入り口右側のディスプレイ棚
3. 店内最奥部から見たイートイン客席
4. 入り口側ケーキ売り場から奥のイートイン客席方向を見る
5. 入り口に面したケーキ売り場のショーケース

1. A night view of the facade from the street
2. A view of the display shelves in the cake shop area
3. A view of the eat-in seating from the inner part
4. A view from the cake shop area to the eat-in seating
5. A view of the showcase in the cake shop area

地元密着型のクラシックモダンなケーキカフェ | Patisserie Cafe **PREMIER**

プルミエール
大阪・日本橋

Nihonbashi, Osaka
Designer: Hiroki Michishita
Photographer: Seiryo Yamada

設 計：道下浩樹デザイン事務所
施 工：オムニコーポレーション

1

流木に導かれた居心地の良いデザイン

大阪の日本橋の外れにできたプルミエールは、28歳の若いオーナーが、地元に密着し愛されるケーキカフェを目標にオープンしたものである。インテリアは、平凡さ、温かさ、優しさ、飽きのこないデザインをコンセプトに、モダンさをほんの少しアレンジし、自然素材を使うことによって居心地の良さを追求している。
客席数22の小さな店内を特徴づけているのは、内部空間のあちこちを飾っている流木である。設計者とオーナーは二人で海岸に出かけ、漂着したまま打ち捨てられた流木を集めてきて素材として使用した。目に見えない自然の力で造形された流木は、素朴でシンプルな空間に不思議な彩りを与えている。

Premier

Premier, located on the outskirts of Nihonbashi in Osaka, was opened by a 28-year-old with the aim of creating a cake cafe firmly established in the community and beloved by customers. The designer aimed for an ordinary, warm and friendly look of which customers will never tire. Small touches of the modern were used along with natural materials to create a comfortable space. Driftwood was placed here and there to accent the small interior, which seats 22. The designer and owner went to the coast together to gather the pieces. Molded by nature, driftwood lends the space unrefined, simple and mysterious color.

1. 入り口左側のケーキケースわきから見た奥の客席
2. 道路から見た外観夜景。折り畳み戸は道路側に開け放つことができる
3. 道路に面した左側客席からケーキケースとカウンター席方向を見る
4. 入り口右側の客席。左側壁面に流木が飾られている

1. A view from the cake showcase to the inner part seating
2. A night view of the facade
3. A view of the cake showcase and counter seating
4. A view of the right side seating with driftwood

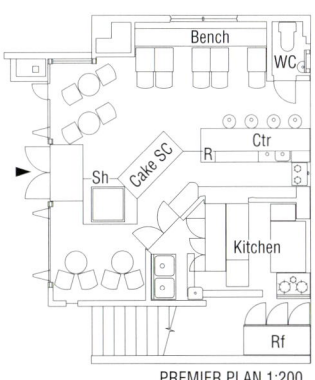

PREMIER PLAN 1:200

CAFE COMPLEXES 35

フレンチスタイルのパティスリーサロン・ド・テ

ル・プティ・ブドン

東京・代官山

Patisserie-salon De Thé **LE PETIT BEDON**

Hachiyama-cho, Tokyo
Designer: Kazuko Fujie
Photographer: Satoshi Asakawa

設 計：藤江和子アトリエ
施 工：竹中工務店
　　　　松坂屋　共立建築

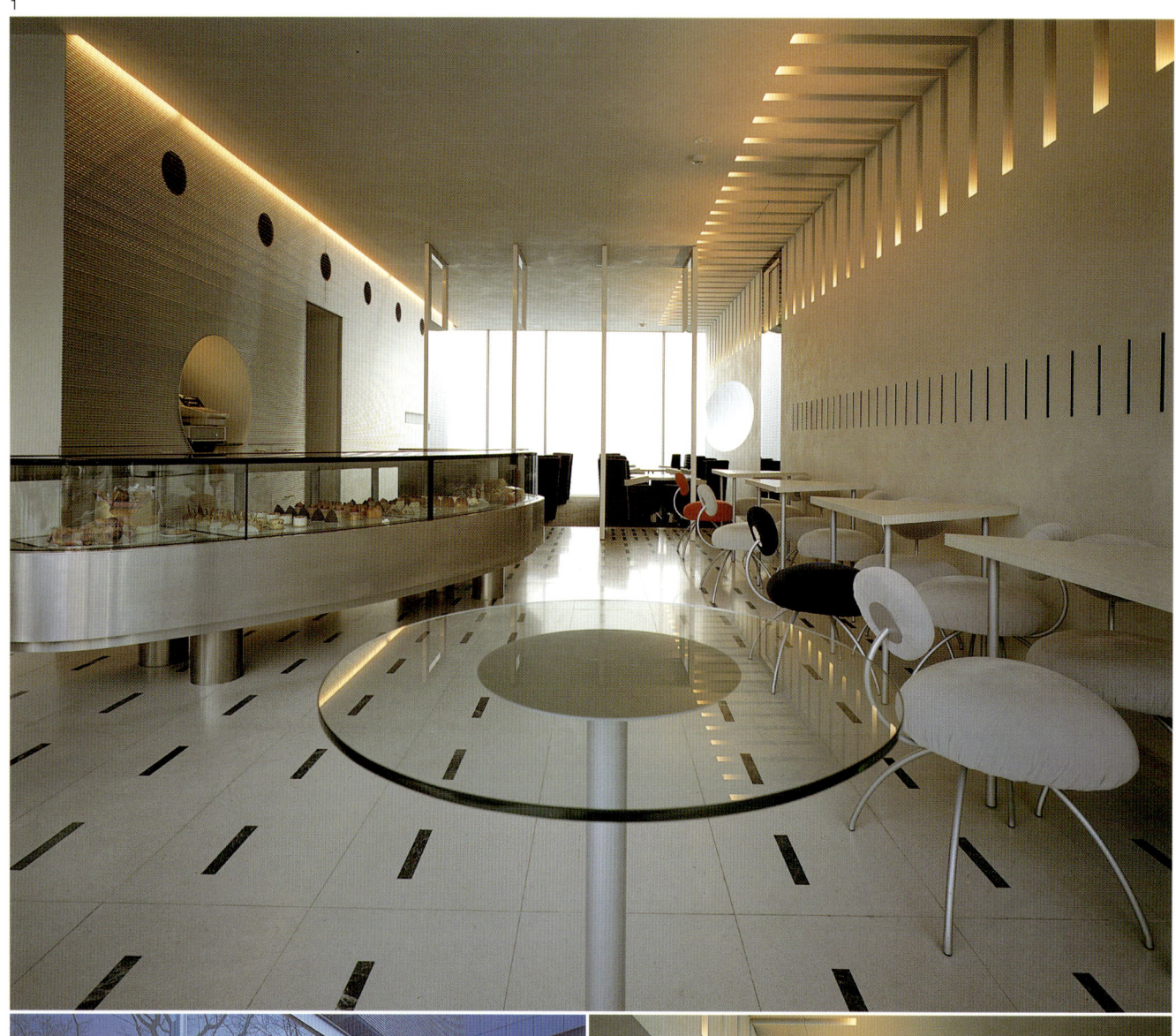

1. 道路側に面した客席から奥方向を見る。奥のパーティションは折り畳まれた状態
2. 道路からセットバックしたファサード。右下は地下レストランのトップライト部分
3. パーティションで仕切られた状態の奥の客席
4. 入り口から見た店内客席。建築デザインを生かした開放的な空間構成

1. A view from the street side seating to the inner part
2. A view of the facade facing the basement skylight
3. A view of the inner part seating with folding partition
4. A view from the entrance to the cake showcase and seating

建築の特性を生かしたインテリア

東京・代官山のヒルサイドテラスは、建築家・槇文彦が新たな街づくりの一環として取り組み、30年に渡り、各棟が次々と建設されてきた。その1棟として完成したヒルサイドウエストに「ル・プティ・ブドン」はある。1階がケーキカフェ、地下1階がフレンチレストランである。
1階ケーキカフェの空間は、通りに面した前面と後側の開口部が全面ガラス張りで、自然光が両側から透過する直方体の空間であった。この伸びやかで明るいという建築的な特質を損なうことなく、カフェとしての機能を挿入することがインテリアの重要なテーマとなった。そのため、床面パターンの濃度を徐々に上げてゆき、最後に"反転"するという手法がとられた。また、透過する空間で唯一視線を遮るものとして、ライトグレーと黒に塗り分けられたパーティションが中央部の奥に設けられた。

Le Petit Bedon

Architect Maki Fumihiko undertook the commercial and residential development Hillside Terrace in Daikanyama, Tokyo, 30 years ago as one example of his new concept of planning, and buildings have been sprouting up there one after another ever since. Le Petit Bedon is located in the building known as Hillside West. The first floor is a cake cafe, and the first underground floor a French restaurant. In the first-floor cake cafe, the space between the street-facing front and the back is built entirely of glass windows, and it constitutes a rectangular parallelepiped that admits sunlight from both sides. An important theme of the interior design was incorporating the functions of a cafe into this space without doing damage to its architectural characteristics of comfort and brightness. So the floor pattern was created so that its concentration increases gradually and then reverses, and a partition painted light gray and black was set up in the center to obstruct the sole continuous line of sight.

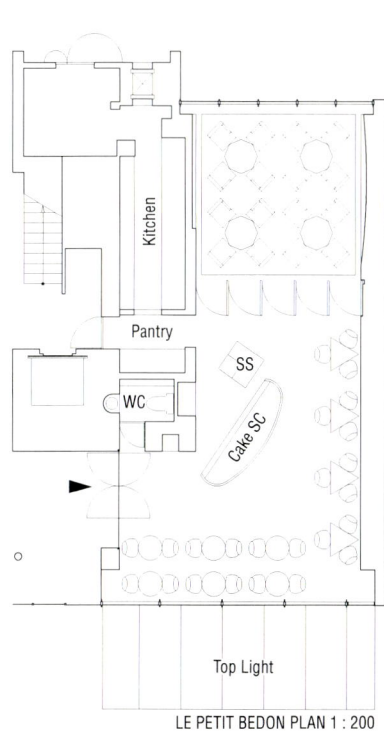

LE PETIT BEDON PLAN 1 : 200

CAFE COMPLEXES 37

有名店の新しいブランドによるケーキ＆カフェ

Cake & Italian Restaurant C³ Ashiya

シーキューブ 芦屋店

芦屋・船戸町

Funado-cho, Ashiya
Designer: Hisatomi Fujikawa
Photographer: Minoru Karamatsu

設 計：エディフス・アソシエイツ
施 工：淀工芸

1

自然の素材と流線形によるデザイン

JR芦屋駅とペデストリアンデッキで直接つながっている商業ビルの1階と2階にシーキューブは計画された。道路に面した入り口のある1階が厨房とケーキ売り場であり、ペデストリアンデッキからの入り口を持つ2階がカフェレストランとなっている。空間デザインのコンセプトは「自然の素材と流線ライン」であり、同時にモダンデザインの大きな特質である透明性を実現することにも力が注がれた。なかでも二つの入り口から互いの階が見通せないマイナスをカバーするため、1、2階を結ぶ階段部分のデザインに大きなウエートが置かれた。美しい曲線を描くステンレス製の階段フレームには、ガラスの踏み板が取り付けられ、階段を上下する来客に空中を浮遊するような感覚を与えている。

C³

C³ (read C cube) is located on the first and second floors of a commercial building directly connected to Japan Rail's Ashiya Station by a pedestrian deck. The first floor has an entrance facing the road and contains the kitchen and a cake counter, and the second floor, with an entrance from the pedestrian deck, contains a cafe and restaurant. The design concept of the space is summed up in the phrase natural materials and streamlining. Great emphasis was also placed on achieving the transparency that is an important characteristic of modern design. To make up for the deficiency of each entrance providing an unobstructed view only of its respective floor, great emphasis was placed on the design of the stairs connecting the two floors. The steps installed in the beautifully curved stainless steel staircase are made of glass, giving customers climbing up and down the feeling they are floating in midair.

---

1. 1階ケーキ売り場と2階カフェレストランをつなぐ流線型の階段。踏み板は強化ガラス製
2. 2階カフェの階段わきから見た客席
3. 2階ペデストリアンデッキ側入り口から見たカフェレストランのサービスカウンターと厨房

1. A view of the staircase on the first floor cake shop
2. A view from the staircase side to the second floor cafe and restaurant
3. A view from the pedestrian deck side entrance to the second floor seating

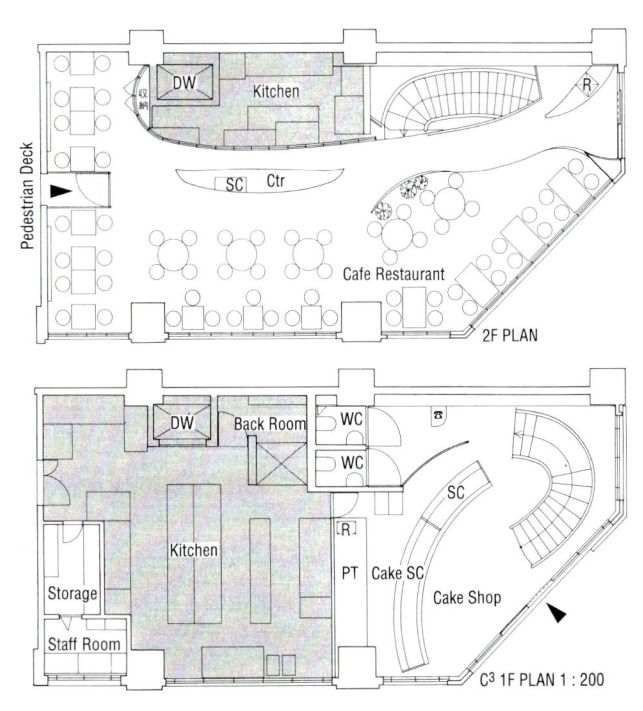

CAFE COMPLEXES

菓子メーカーが経営する観光地のカフェ

Cafe & Confectionery **FRESCA**

フレスカ 三万石猪苗代店

福島・猪苗代町

Inawashiro-machi, Fukushima
Designer: Kuninori Yamada
Photographer: Keisuke Miyamoto

設 計：山田邦史
施 工：佐藤工業郡山支店

1

1. 南側に配された中庭のテラス席から
   カフェ棟を見る
2. 東側ショップ棟の入り口から見た
   菓子売り場
3. 東側から見た外観夜景。カフェ棟は
   外壁が頂部までガラス張り

1. A view of the terrace seating and cafe wing
   from the east
2. A view of the confectionery shop area
   in the shop wing
3. A night view of the facade from the east

眺望と周囲の恵まれた自然を生かす

東北地方有数のリゾート地・猪苗代湖の湖を望む景観地にできた「フレスカ」は，この地域でも指折りの菓子メーカーが自社の製品を観光客にアピールするとともに，企業のイメージアップを図るために出店したもの。計画に際しては，観光地にありがちな土産物屋的な店舗ではなく，シンプルでモダンな形態が望まれた。

道路から見て右側の八角形のシリンダー状の建物は，菓子の日本的なパッケージのイメージを表現したものであり，内部は菓子売り場となっている。左側の大きなガラス面の外壁を持つ建物内部はカフェであり，両者をつなぐかたちで，ガラス張りの開口部に囲まれたテラス席の中庭が配された。自然志向のメニューはヘルシーなヨーグルトがメーンであり，中庭で栽培されている新鮮なハーブを使ったメニューも用意されている。

Fresca

Fresca was built at Inawashiro, one of the few resorts in the Tohoku region, in a scenic spot that commands a view of Lake Inawashiro. It is the creation of a leading regional confectionery maker that sought to offer its products to tourists and polish its corporate image. The cafe was planned as a simple, modern establishment distinct from the typical souvenir shops one finds in tourist areas. The confectionery sales counter is found inside an 8-sided, cylindrical building, which stands on the right when viewed from the road. The structure is a representation of the packages Japanese sweets usually come in. The building to the left, with a large, glass, external wall, is a cafe. A glass-enclosed garden with terrace seating connects the two buildings. Healthy yogurt is the main item on the natural foods heavy menu, which includes dishes that use fresh herbs from the garden.

4. カフェの入り口左側客席を厨房側から見る
5. 南側から見た正面夜景。左がカフェ，右が菓子ショップ

4. A view of the cafe seating from the kitchen side
5. An evening view of the facade from the south

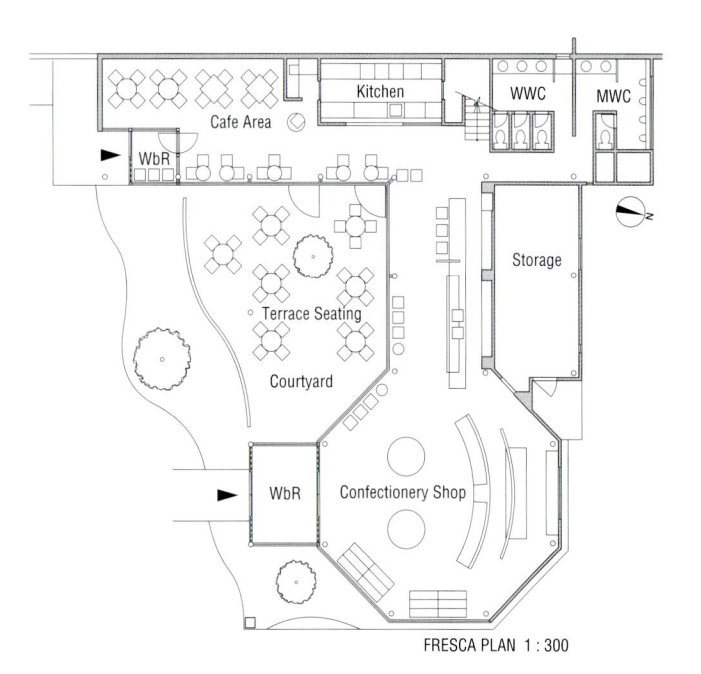

FRESCA PLAN 1 : 300

京都の焼き菓子老舗によるシュークリーム店

Cream Puff **CREME DE LA CREME**

クレーム デ ラ クレーム

京都・烏丸通

Karasuma-doori, Kyoto
Designer: GK kyoto
Photographer: Hiroshi Fujiwara

設 計： GK京都
　　　　GK設計大阪事務所ほか
施 工： 大岩建設工業

1

ショップインファクトリーがコンセプト

明治時代から130年間，焼き和菓子を作り続けてきた京都の老舗が，歴史と伝統を生かして始めたシュークリームのショップとカフェ。1階が工場とシュークリームの売り場，2階がカフェである。周囲はオフィスビルの建ち並ぶ無機質な街並みであるため，外観は新鮮さを持ちながら時を経るにしたがって味の出る建築デザインが志向された。
1階のインテリアは，工場そのものがショップというコンセプトからステンレス製のケーキケースとカウンターを連続して配し，工場とショップの一体感を演出。また，2階の床，壁，天井などの空間を構成する要素は，柔らかな質感のタイルや，しっくい塗りなどの天然素材をメーンに使用，それらと対比的なステンレスやアルミなどの金属素材とガラス素材を要所に配し，自然光やライティングで光を反射，または透過させてその存在感や素地の美しさを強調している。

Créme de la Créme

Créme de la Créme is a shop and cafe built by a long-standing Kyoto confectioner that began making baked wagashi (Japanese confectioneries) 130 years ago in the Meiji era. It serves as a showroom for the confectioner's history and traditions. The first floor holds a factory and cream puff sales counter and the second floor is a cafe. Because Créme de la Créme is situated amid a lifeless row of office buildings, the architect sought to design an exterior that would be fresh and at the same time grow in appeal with the passage of time.The interior of the first floor integrates the ideas of factory and shop, placing stainless steel cake cases and counters in a row. Materials with a natural feel such as soft-textured tile and plaster are the main elements used in the second story's floors, walls and ceiling. To provide contrast, glass and metals such as stainless steel and aluminum were placed in important spots throughout. They reflect artificial light and admit sunlight to emphasize the beauty, substantiality and texture of the tile and plaster.

1. 1階入り口側から見たシュークリーム売り場。奥が工場
2. スキップアップした2階カフェの道路側客席
3. 1階ショップのシュークリームショーケース
4. 道路から見たファサード夕景
5. 2階道路側客席から吹き抜けを通して奥のパントリー方向を見る

1. A view of the cream puff shop on the first floor
2. A view of the street side seating on the second floor
3. A view of the cream puff showcase on the first floor
4. An evening view of the facade
5. A view from the street side seating to the pantry side on the second floor

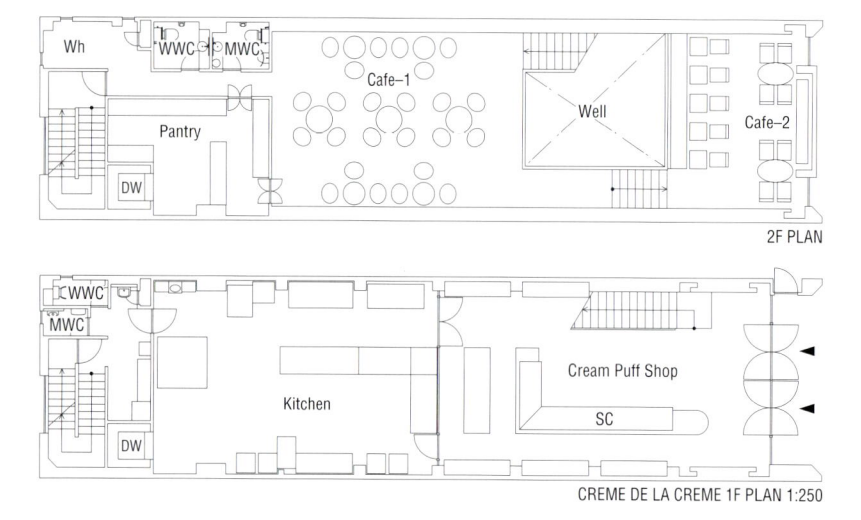

CREME DE LA CREME 1F PLAN 1:250

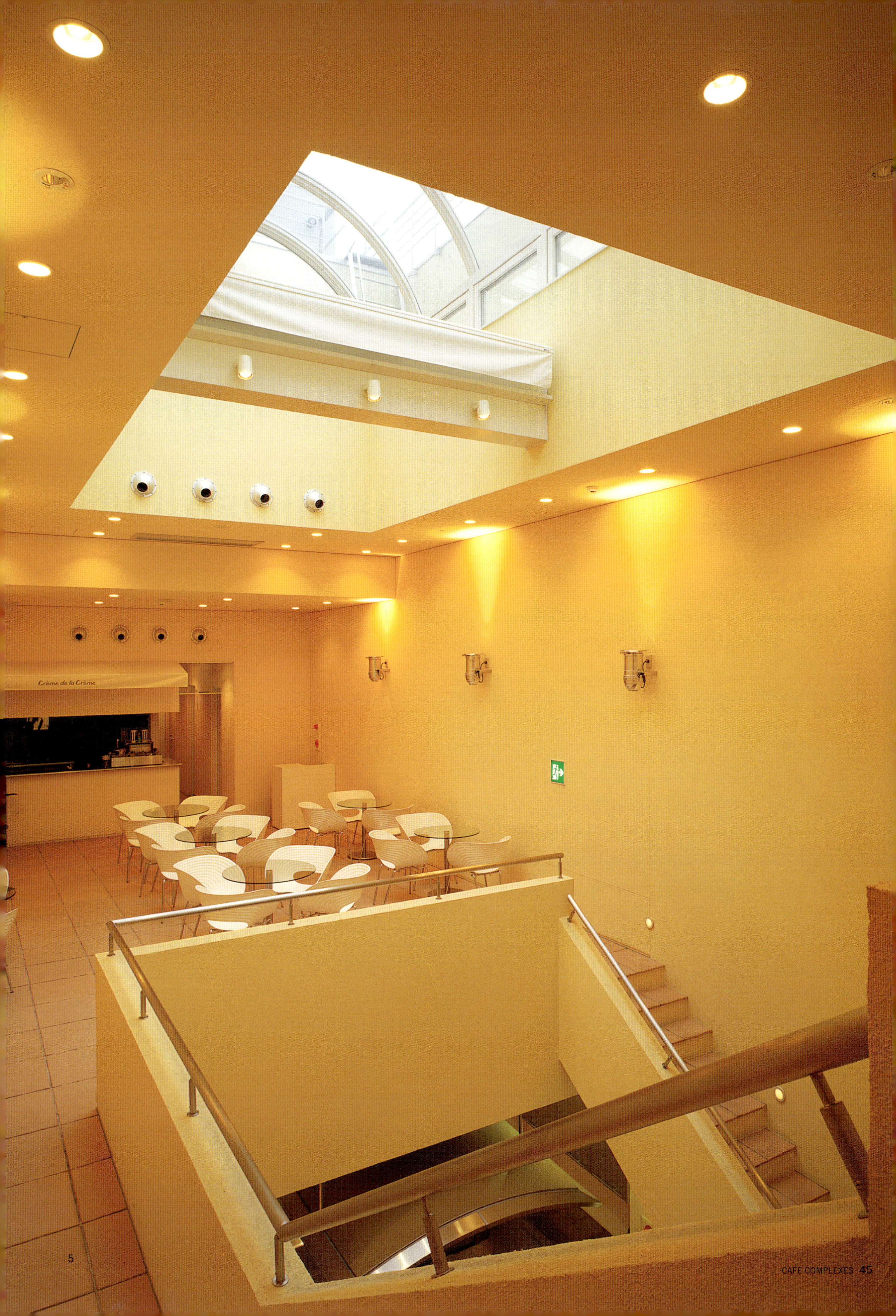

5

本格的なイタリアンデリ＆カフェ

A.D.K.
東京・南青山

Italian Deli & Cafe **A.D.K.**

Minami-aoyama, Tokyo
Designer: United Pacifics
Photographer: Kaku Ootaki

設 計：ユナイテッドパシフィックス
施 工：万造工務所

本場・イタリアのデリを再現

東京・青山の裏通りにできたこの「A.D.K.」は、高級な機械式腕時計を扱う企業の店舗ビルの一角を改装してオープンした。日本に今までなかった本格的なイタリアンデリの店をつくるというのが目的で、コーヒーメーカーなどの厨房機器はイタリアに発注し、また、料理は無農薬の食材を一流のシェフが調理するなど、本格的な味を追求している。ファサードデザインはなじみやすいイタリアのデリを再現したものであり、また、1階入り口まわりのテラス的なカウンター席、窓外のグリーンを借景にした内部のベンチ席など半屋外的な感覚を演出している。利用形態はテイクアウトとイートインが半々、客層は20～30歳代が中心で、女性客が60％を占める。

A.D.K.

A.D.K. is located on an Aoyama, Tokyo, back street in a remodeled corner of a retail building of a high-grade mechanical wristwatch company. Seeking to create the first authentic Italian deli in Japan, the owner ordered a coffee maker and other kitchen equipment from Italy and hired a top chef who uses organic ingredients. The shop recreates the friendly facade of an Italian deli, and the terracelike counter seating around the first-floor entrance and bench seating that takes advantage of the scenic green outside the windows combine to produce a sensation of being outdoors. A.D.K.'s business is evenly split between takeout and eat-in. Most of its customers are in their 20s and 30s, with 60 percent of them women.

1. 1階入り口右側のベンチ席からデリショーケース方向を見る
2. 奥の吹き抜けラセン階段から見た1階と地下1階の客席
3. イタリアのデリを再現したファサード

1. A view from the bench seating to the deli showcase on the first floor
2. A view from the spiral stairs to the first floor and first basement floor
3. A view of the facade imaging Italian deli shop

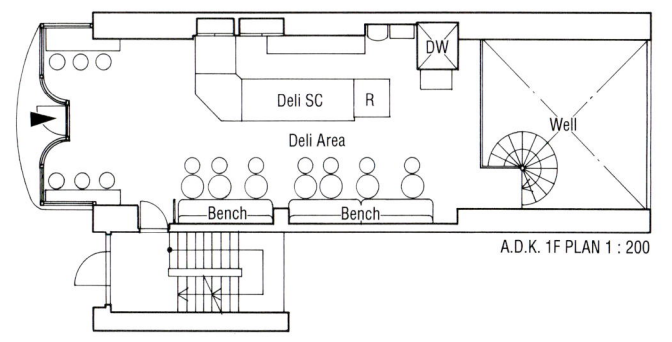

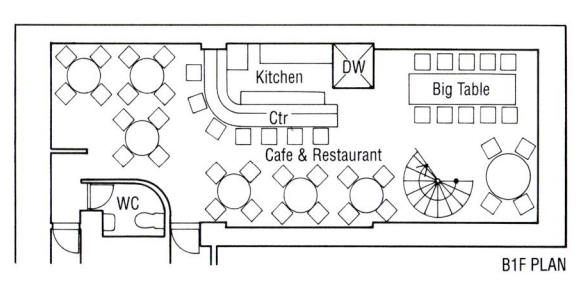

サンドイッチを主力としたデリ&カフェ

Cafe & Deli **NEW YORK DELI**

ニューヨークデリ
大阪・南船場

Minami-senba, Osaka
Designer: Mitsuhiro Mizutani
Photographer: Seiryo Yamada

設計：クル
施工：キクスイ

1. 地下街に面したファサード
2. 店内左奥のデリショーケースを客席から見る
3. 入り口左側から見た店内全景

1. A view of the facade facing the underground shopping center passage
2. A view of the deli showcase from the inner part seating
3. A view of the whole interior from the left side entrance

食材が主役のシンプルなモノトーン空間

大阪の新しい商業立地として、おしゃれなショップが次々とできている南船場に20〜30歳代の女性を対象として、地域にふさわしいニューヨークスタイルのカフェ＆デリがオープンした。厳選された食材や総菜を自由にオーダーメイドできるサンドイッチが売り物であり、ニューヨークでは普通にある業態だが、大阪では初の試みである。
食材が主役となることを目指したインテリアデザインは、できるだけシンプルな構成とされ、モノトーンの色彩により食材が引き立ち、温かみのある照明によって楽しい会話が弾むよう配慮されている。1日の客回転数の多さと客の約70％が女性ということから、立地条件が整えばチェーン化が可能であるという判断で、次の出店への準備が進められている。

New York Deli

New York Deli is located in Minami-senba, a new commercial area in Osaka that has been the site of a series of fashionable shop openings. The owners sought to create a New York style deli that would be appropriate to the region and appeal to women in their 20s and 30s. New York Deli sells sandwiches made to order with carefully selected ingredients and condiments. Such shops are common in New York, but this one represents a new experiment in Osaka. The monotone interior was designed simply to give prominence to the sandwich ingredients, with warm lighting added to create an atmosphere suitable to pleasant conversation. In consideration of the large number of daily customers and the fact that 70 percent of them are women, the owners are preparing to open another outlet, and are considering expanding into a full-fledged chain if they can find suitable locations.

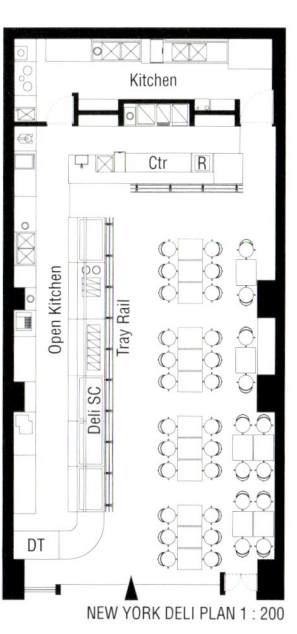

NEW YORK DELI PLAN 1 : 200

中庭を取り囲んだベーカーリー・カフェレストラン　　Bakery Cafe Restaurant **632**

632
東京・神宮前

Jingumae, Tokyo
Designer: Yutetsu Ihara
Photographer: Yasuo Sadayama

設 計： 井原勇哲ほか
施 工： 前田建設工業ほか

誰でも入れるユニバーサルなデザイン

東京・原宿周辺はファッショナブルなカフェやレストランがひしめく、競合の激しい地域である。原宿の裏通りにできた「632」は、石油、不動産、飲食店という三つの事業を展開している企業が経営しており、以前は同社の社員寮があった場所を再開発したもの。

建築デザインは、中庭をコの字形に取り囲んだ形態とされ、右端にある入り口からベーカリー＆デリ売り場、カフェ、カウンターバー、ダイニングという順番に配されている。どのエリアからも中庭のテラス席が見える店内は、クライアントの要望によって、障害者だけを対象としたバリアフリーでなく、車椅子やベビーカー、老人、そして中庭にはペットも入れる広い意味でのユニバーサルデザインが実現された。

632

Many fashionable cafes and restaurants compete for customers in the area around Harajuku, Tokyo. 632 was opened on a Harajuku back street by a company developing oil, real estate and restaurant businesses. The building is a redeveloped former dormitory for the company's employees. The courtyard is surrounded by the U-shaped building. From the right-end entrance, customers encounter first a bakery and deli counter, then a cafe, counter bar and dining room. The courtyard's terrace seating is visible from anywhere inside. To meet customer demand, a universal-use design was chosen for 632, making it barrier free for easy access by the disabled, wheelchairs, strollers and the elderly. Pets are allowed in the courtyard.

1. 道路側から見たファサード夜景
2. 板貼りのガーデンテラス席をカウンターバー側から見る
3. カフェとレストランの間に設けられたカウンターバー
4. カフェ客席からレジカウンターとデリのコーナーを見る
5. 入り口から見たレジカウンターおよび中2階への階段まわり

1. A night view of the facade from the street
2. A view of the garden terrace from the bar side
3. A view of the bar counter between the cafe and the restaurant
4. A view from the cafe seating to the cashier and deli showcases
5. A view from the entrance to the cashier and stairs

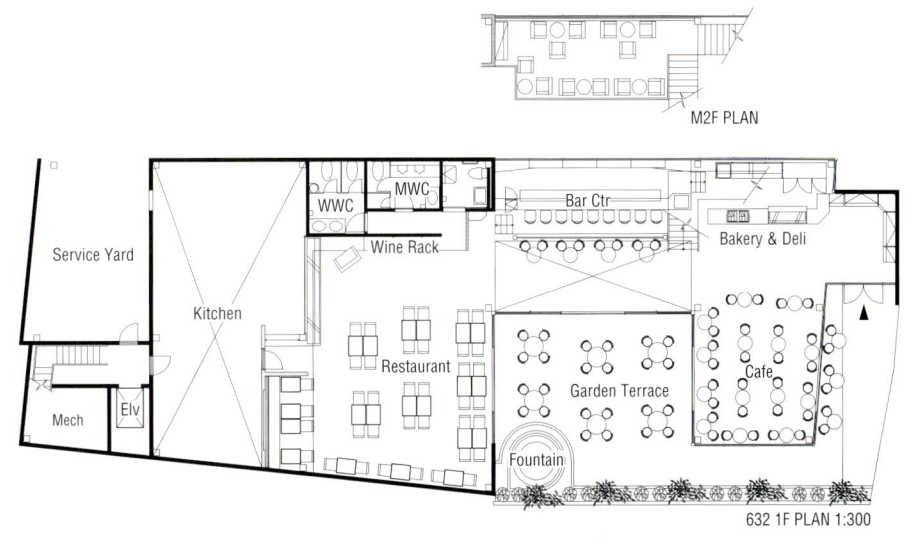

632 1F PLAN 1:300

ベーカリーカフェ&プロダクトデザインショップ　　Bakery Cafe & Goods Shop **CASLON**

キャスロン

仙台・紫山

Murasakiyama, Sendai
Designer: Shigemitsu Hara
Photographer: Yoshio Shiratori

設 計：ジョイントセンター
施 工：センケンホーム

ショップ全体の一体感を重視

東北地方の中心・仙台市の郊外、丘陵地の頂部に「キャスロン」はある。この地域は近くにニュータウンや図書館、ホテルなども建設されている開発地であるが、周囲は緑に恵まれた環境である。店舗のコンセプトは、マスプロダクションでは不可能な食べ物、サービス、プロダクト製品を提供していこうということで、天然酵母、天然塩を使ったパンやピザが製造され、また、この店のために開発された食器類などの小物類がグッズショップで売られてる。

店内はそれぞれのエリアを分断することなく、素材、色彩、照明を統一してショップ全体の統一感を出すようにデザインされている。また、季節によっては背後の庭に面したカフェの2面のガラス引き戸を開け放つことにより、開放感に溢れたオープンカフェにもなる。

Caslon

Caslon sits atop a hilly area in a suburb of Sendai city, in the central part of the Tohoku region. A new town, a library and a hotel are being developed in the area, but it is surrounded by a green, natural environment. The concept behind this bakery cafe and shop is offering food, service and products that would be impossible to mass-produce. Caslon serves bread and pizza made using natural yeast and salt, and its shop sells tableware designed for the cafe and other small articles. The shop is not divided into separate areas, and the same raw materials, coloring and illumination are used throughout to give it a unified feel. In the warmer seasons, two sliding glass doors to the garden in back can be opened to create an open cafe.

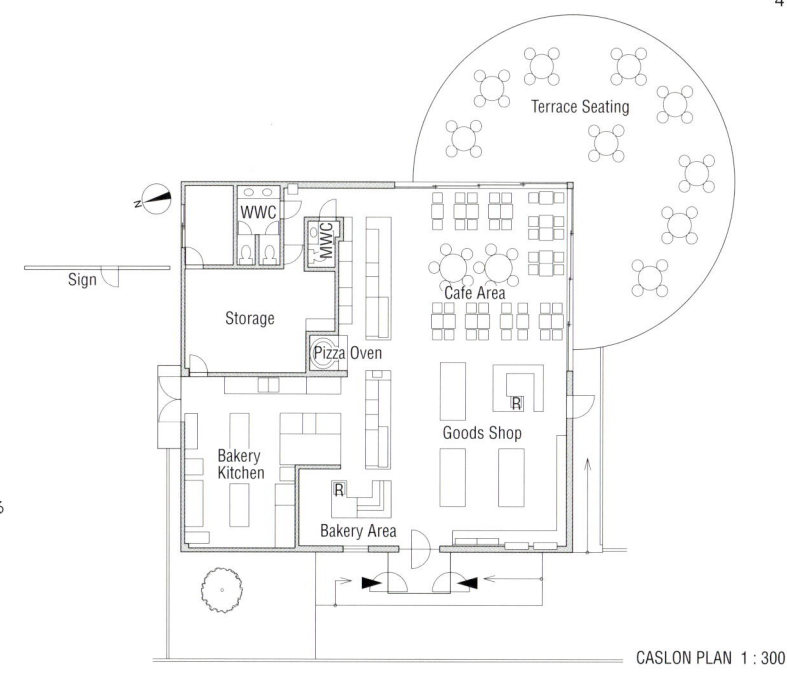

1. 西側から見たファサード。建物の後ろ側に屋外テラスが広がる
2. プロダクトデザインコーナーからカフェ客席と屋外のテラス席を見る
3. 入り口から左側のベーカリーコーナーとレジカウンターを見る
4. 入り口右側のプロダクトデザインコーナー内部

1. A view of the facade from the west
2. A view from the cafe seating to the outdoor terrace
3. A view of the bakery showcases and cashier from the entrance
4. A view of the products design shop area

CASLON PLAN 1 : 300

| 郊外型ベーカーリー＋カフェレストラン | Bakery & Cafe Restaurant **PAIN DE QUERCY** |

パン・ド・ケルシー

高崎・上小塙町

Kamikobana-machi, Takasaki
Designer: Takashi Shimizu
Photographer: Masaharu Nakatsuka

設 計：ドス・パートナーシップ
施 工：清水

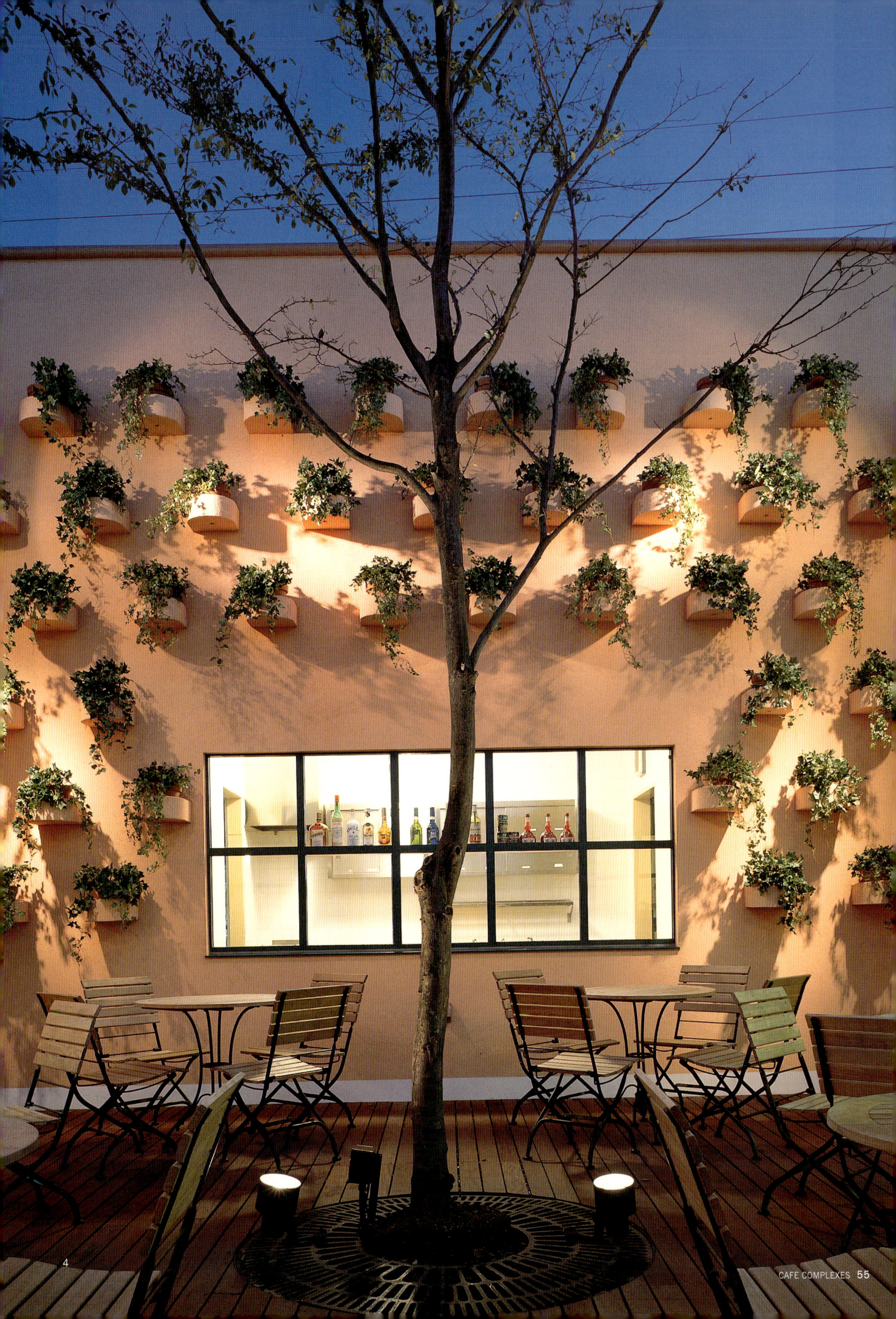

4

都会的雰囲気のパティオを中心とする

関東平野の交通の要衝・高崎市の西側、最近ではいろいろなショップができ始めたが、周囲にはまだ田圃や畑が残っている通りに「パン・ド・ケルシー」は完成した。高崎市内に6店舗のベーカリーを経営する企業の初めてのロードサイド型ベーカリーカフェレストランである。

店づくりに際してのテーマは、店名の由来であるフランス南西部のケルシー地方の素朴さと優雅さを、都会的なモダンさとミックスすることであった。そこで、周囲の環境とは違った雰囲気を創出するため、レストランとベーカリーの間にパティオを設け、店内のどこからもパティオが見えるように計画された。また、空間全体の色調と素材に関しては、清潔感と優しさ、温かさが感じられるものが採り入れられた。

Pain de Quercy

Recently a variety of shops have begun to open in the western part of the city of Takasaki, a key transportation point on the Kanto Plain. But Pan de Quercy is located on a street on the area's outskirts in a place that still has rice paddies and fields. A company that manages six bakeries in Takasaki opened this establishment as its first roadside bakery, cafe restaurant. The restaurant's theme is mixing urban modernity with the simplicity and elegance of Quercy, its namesake region in southwestern France. So to create an atmosphere that contrasts with Pan de Quercy's surroundings, a patio was installed between the cafe restaurant and bakery, and the design ensured that it is visible from anywhere inside. Coloring and materials that convey cleanliness, gentleness and warmth were adopted for the entire space.

1. 北西側から見た外観夜景
2. 道路側ウインドーから見た東側カフェレストラン棟の内部客席
3. カフェレストラン客席内部からパティオのテラス席方向を見る
4. カフェレストラン棟とベーカリー棟に挟まれた路地から中庭のパティオを見る
5. パティオ側入り口から見たベーカリー内部
6. 入り口側から見たカフェ客席

1. A night view of the facade from the northwest
2. A view of the cafe restaurant through the window from the street
3. A view from the cafe restaurant seating to the terrace on the patio
4. A view of the patio from the street side
5. A view of the bakery from the patio side entrance
6. A view of the cafe restaurant seating from the entrance side

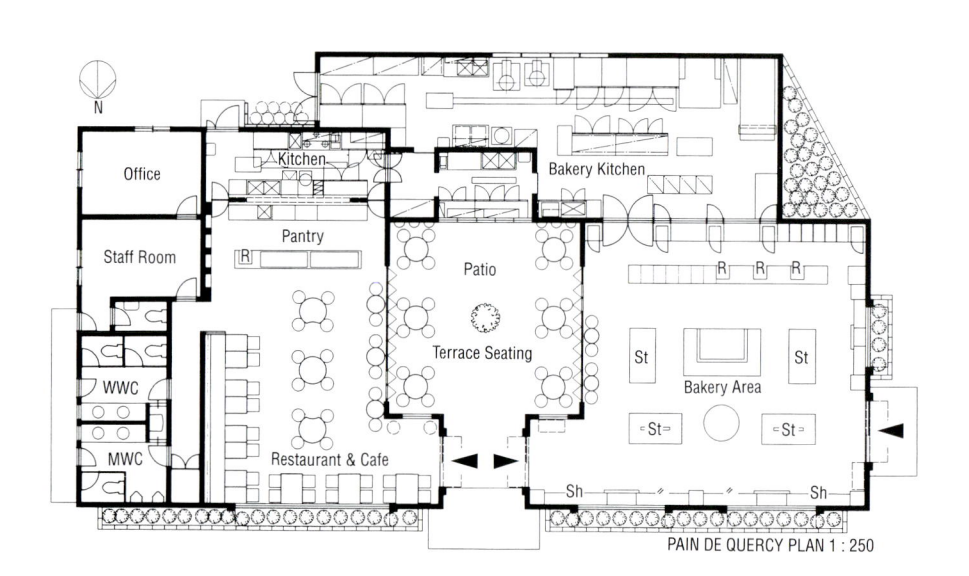

PAIN DE QUERCY PLAN 1 : 250

SHOP DESIGN SERIES
CHAPTER 2

CAFES & TEAROOMS

| カフェテリアを併設した自家焙煎珈琲店 | Coffee Shop **SAKURA-JAYA** |

櫻茶屋
徳島・北沖洲

Kita-okinosu, Tokushima
Designer: Yuji Sumitomo
Photographer: Sai Kawamoto

設 計：マス・アソシエイティ
施 工：島出建築事務所

1

1. 南側から見た入り口まわり外観夕景
2. 右奥トイレ前より客席を通してラウンジ方向を見る

1. An evening view of the entrance from the south
2. A view from the toilet side to the lounge

自然素材によるダイナミックな空間

四国・徳島市の町外れ、玄関口にあたる場所に「櫻茶屋」はある。周辺には企業団地、中央卸売り市場があり、近年、物流の中心地区として発展してきた。この地域で従来は配送弁当業務、海産物類の卸業務を営んでいた企業が、配送弁当の建物を改装してオープンさせた自家焙煎のコーヒーショップである。ただし、配送弁当の業務と厨房は残され、ランチタイムには、カフェテリア形式の食事が提供される。

店づくりのコンセプトは"人間の五感に響く空間"とされ、木材、レンガ、石材、水、緑などの自然素材を中心に空間は構成されている。店内は中央客席の天井を高くとり、木造の小屋組みトラス構造をそのまま見せて、ダイナミックさを演出。また、カフェテリア席は気候の良い季節にはオープンカフェとなるよう、石畳と植栽によって内と外の境界をなくすような配置が採り入れられた。

Sakura-Jaya

The coffee shop Sakura-Jaya is located on the outskirts of Tokushima in a spot that could be called the entranceway to the city. The area contains business complexes and the central wholesale market, and in recent years it has developed into the city's central distribution district.

The coffee shop, which roasts its own beans, was built by a company that manages marine-products wholesale and boxed-lunch delivery businesses, in a remodeled building formerly used for the latter. The boxed-lunch delivery business and kitchen were left in place, and Sakura-Jaya serves cafeteria-style lunches at midday.

The design concept behind Sakura-Jaya was to use primarily natural materials such as wood, brick, stone, water and plants to compose a space that resonates with the five senses. Inside, the dynamic central seating area has a tall ceiling and contains wooden roof trusses structures whose truss-construction is left visible.

3. 入り口右側のラウンジ席
4. レジ前から見たカフェテリア客席

3. A view of the lounge from the kitchen side
4. A view of the cafeteria seating from the cashier

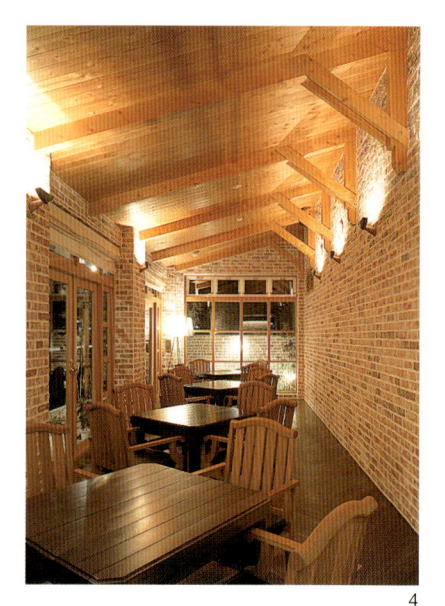

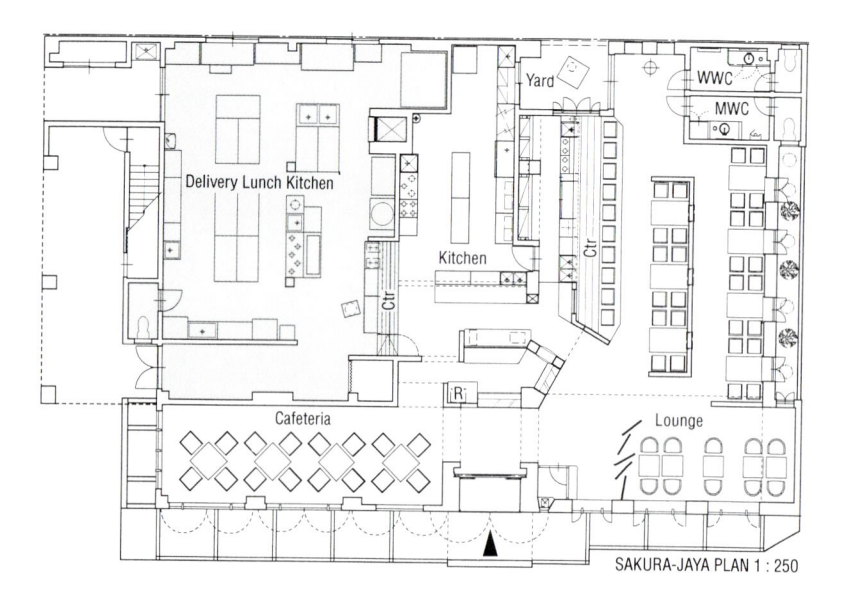

SAKURA-JAYA PLAN 1:250

コーヒーメーカーのアンテナショップ・カフェ	Cafe **NESCAFE**	
# ネスカフェ 神戸・三宮	Goko-doori, Kobe Designer: Yasumasa Yamasaki Photographer: Yasunori Shimomura	設 計： 乃村工芸社 施 工： 竹中工務店　乃村工芸社

1

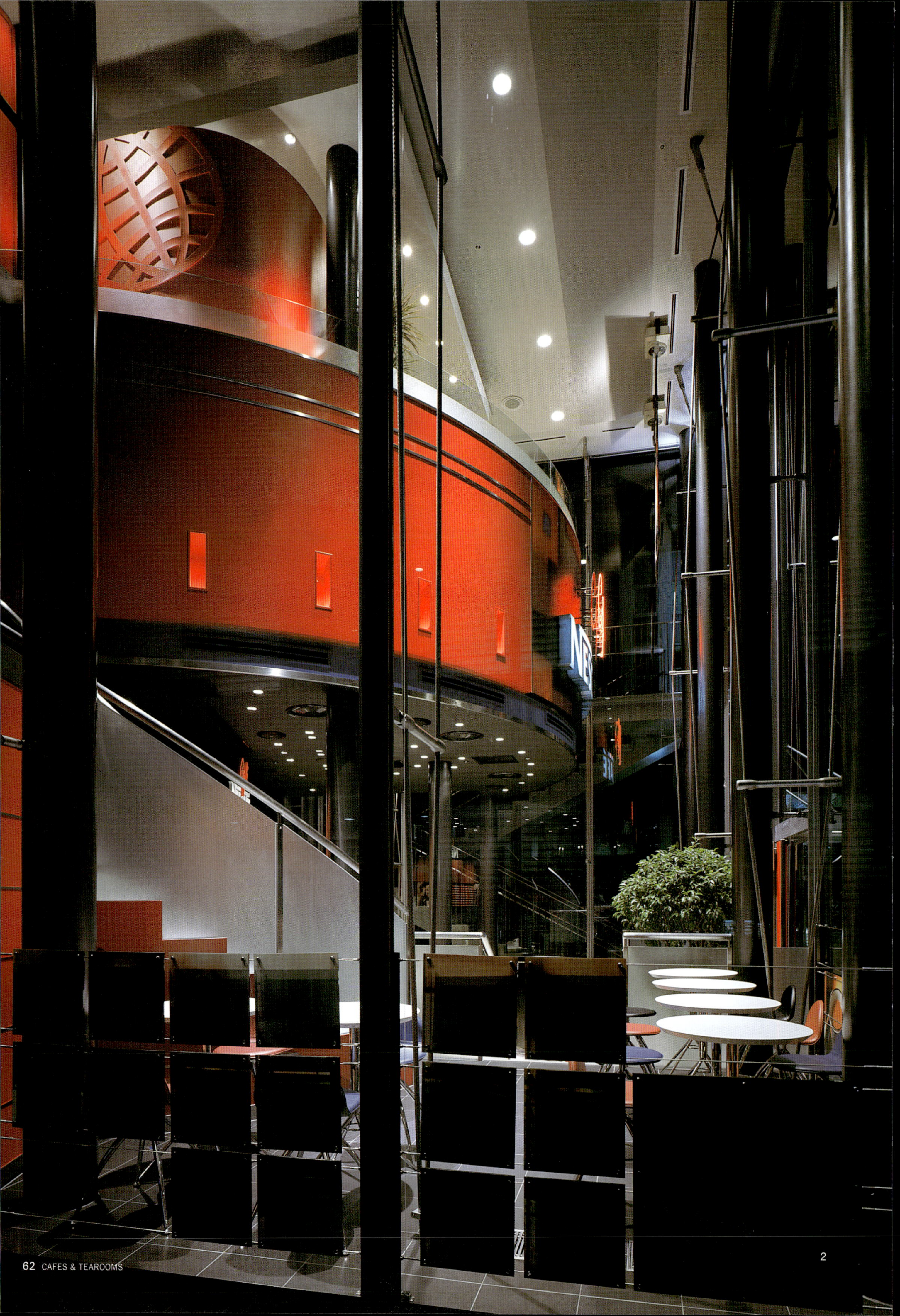

2

インテリアがファサードを兼ねる空間

阪神大震災から復興した神戸の中心部、JR三ノ宮駅の近くに「ネスカフェ」は位置する。経営するネスレ日本の本社が入居しているビルの一角を利用し、別棟としてつくられたもので、日本におけるアンテナショップとしての役割を担っている。ネスカフェブランドのイメージアップとともに、地域の活性化にも貢献しようという目的である。
角地に建ち、三面をガラスで覆われた2階建ての建物は、ガラスを通して外部から内部がすべて見通せることができ、インテリアがそのままファサードとなる特異な構造である。そこで、企業の広告塔の役割を果たしつつ、ターゲットである20代の女性を引きつけるために、店内のデザインは赤と黒の色彩を大胆に使うことが提案された。結果として、モダンでコンテンポラリーな建築形態と色鮮やかなインテリアは、外部に向けてコマーシャルフィルム的なメッセージを放つこととなった。

Nescafe

Nescafe is located near Japan Rail's Sannomiya Station in the center of Kobe, which has been revitalized since the Great Hanshin Earthquake. The cafe is located in a corner lot next to the new headquarters building of the company that manages it, Nescafe Japan, serving as an antenna that helps the firm collect feedback from its customers. The cafe was also intended to help Nescafe Japan polish its brand's image while contributing to the vitalization of the area.
The two-story building is covered in glass on three sides, allowing the interior to be seen from outside and serve as the structure's facade. This design also permits the shop to function as an advertisement for Nescafe. To attract its target demographic of women in their 20s, an audacious coloring scheme of red and black was suggested. The result was a modern structure with a vividly colored interior that broadcasts a commercial message.

1. 道路側から見た外観夜景。3面がガラス張り
2. 側面から見た1階客席と2階への階段まわり
3. ビルのルーフテラスから見た2階部分の外観
4. 2階の大テーブル席

1. A night view of the glass facade from the street
2. A view of the first floor seating and stairs from the street
3. A night view of the second floor facade from the building roof terrace
4. An interior view of the second floor seating

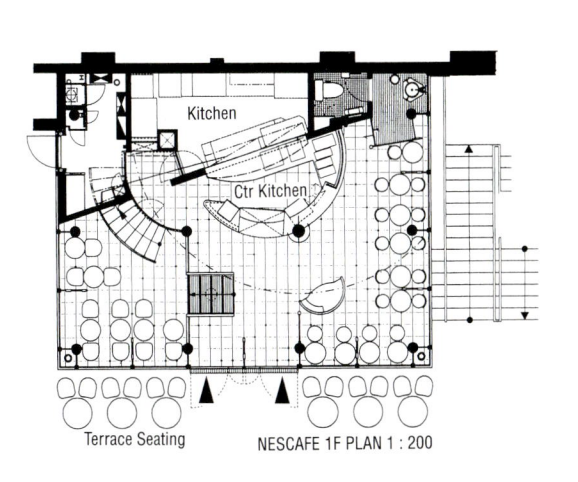

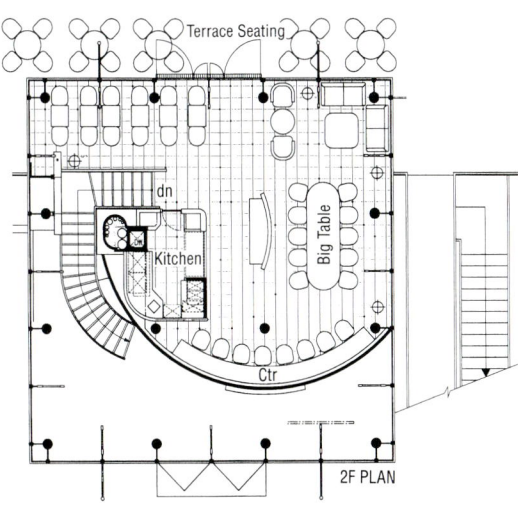

自宅敷地内に建てられたサロン的なカフェ

ロッジ
静岡・沼津市

Cafe **LODGE**

Ebara-cho, Numazu
Designer: bbr
Photographer: Nobuaki Nakagawa

設 計：bbr
施 工：フジヤマ総建

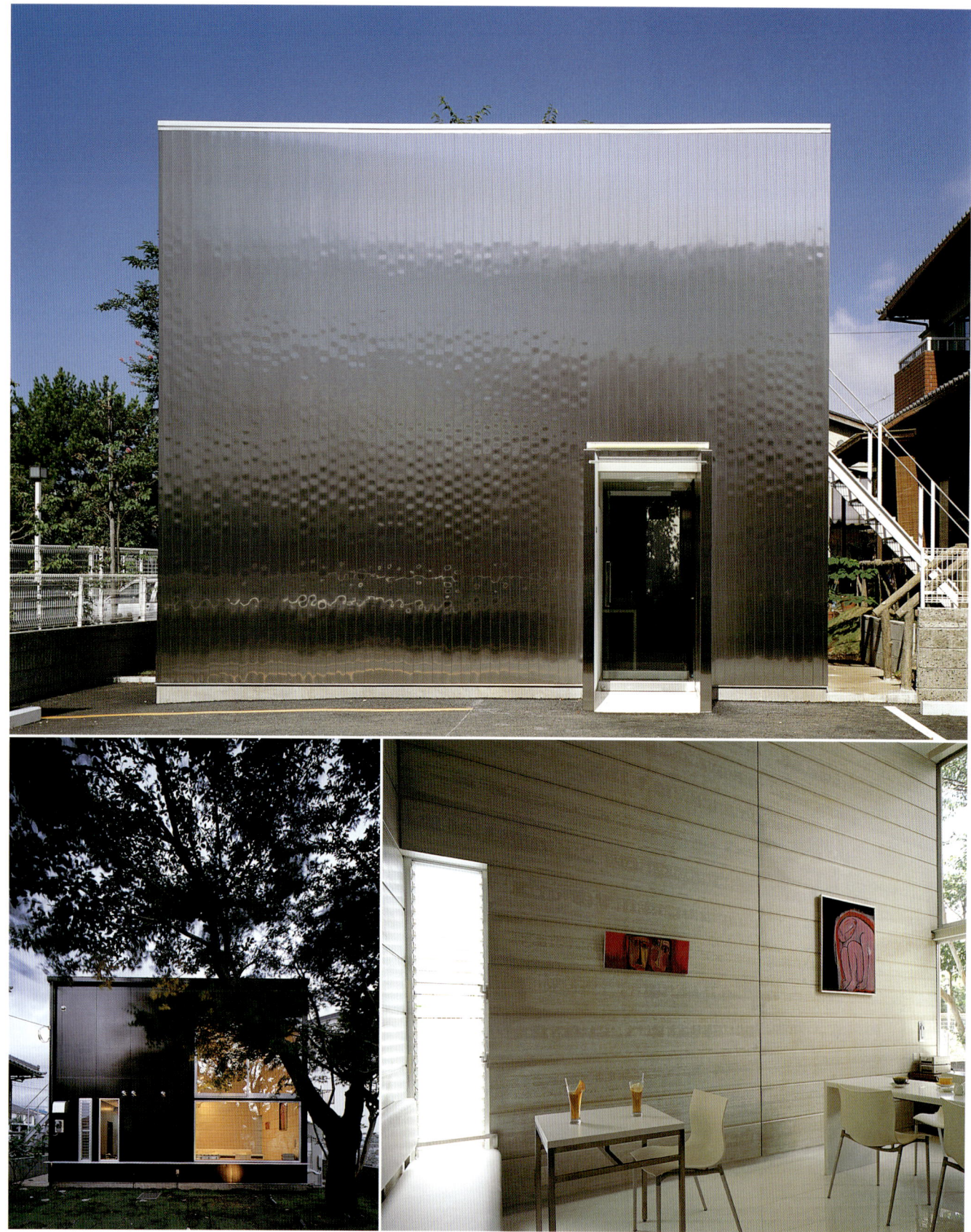

景色を映し出すステンレスのファサード

静岡の地方都市・沼津市の町外れにある住宅街の1角に、この風変わりなカフェはある。20年に渡り山小屋風の喫茶店を経営してきたオーナーが、自宅の敷地に夫婦だけで営業できるサロン的なカフェをつくりたいということで誕生した。
「ロッジ」の最大の特徴は、キューブ状の小さな建物のファサードが厚さ0.4mmのステンレス板で覆われていることで、暑い日差しにさらされると表面が膨張して魚の鱗のような模様が現れ、また、夜になって冷えると外部の照明を反射し、鈍い輝きを放つ。このメタリックな外装とは対照的に、内部は大きなガラス張りの開口部から柔らかな木漏れ日が差し込み、真っ白で光沢のある床に庭の木々が映り込む。

Lodge

The eccentric cafe Lodge is located on a corner of a residential area on the outskirts of Numazu, a city in Shizuoka Prefecture. A man who has been managing a mountain-cabin-style coffee shop for 20 years created the salonlike Lodge on the lot where his home is located because he wanted a cafe he could run with his wife.

The most prominent characteristic of the small, cubic building is the 0.4 mm stainless steel sheets covering the facade. When exposed to the sun's rays, they swell and reveal a fish-scale pattern. At night, when they cool, they softly reflect the external illumination.

Light filters inside onto the lustrous, pure-white floor through the leaves of the trees in the garden and the large glass windows. The reflection of the trees on the floor provides a contrast with the metallic exterior.

1. ステンレスシート貼りの東面ファサード
2. 庭の桜を通して見た西面外観
3. 入り口から見た客席
4. ベンチ席からカウンター席を見る
5. 左奥から見た店内全景

1. A view of the facade from the east
2. A view of the outer wall and window from the west
3. A view of the seating from the entrance
4. A view from the bench seating to the counter seating
5. A whole view of the interior from the inner part

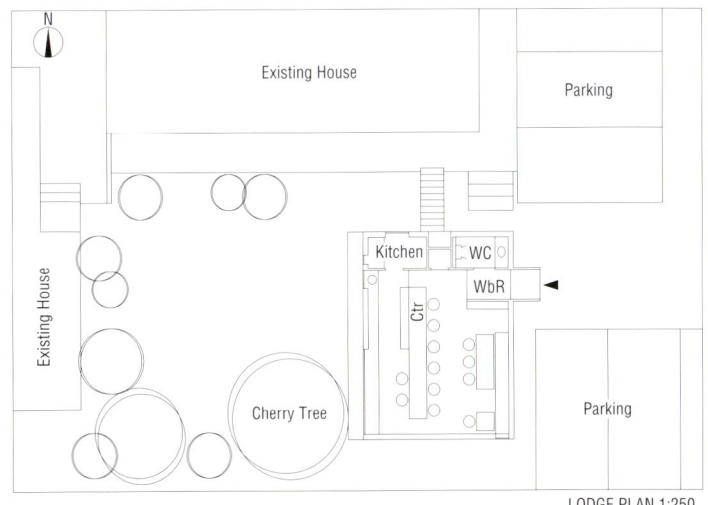

LODGE PLAN 1:250

こだわりを形にした個性的な珈琲専門店 | Cafe **COFFEE CLUB**

珈琲クラブ
香川・高松市

Tahishimo-machi, Takamatsu
Designer: Shinji Kagawa
Photographer: Akira Takahashi

設 計：香川真二＋
　　　　グッドデザインスタジオ
施 工：山本清工務店

1

周囲に存在を主張する外装デザイン

四国・高松市の郊外、自動車道路が整備されて発展しつつある地域に「珈琲クラブ」はオープンした。趣味性の強い人々を対象としたコーヒー専門店ということから、周囲の環境に建物自身がその存在を主張するような、個性的なデザインが建築に求められた。

まず、建物の存在をはっきりと強調するため、道路に面して石積みの塀と緩やかな傾斜の石の階段が設けられ、すぐ背後に建つ建物の外観は、塀の上から見える屋根と入り口上部の庇にポイントが置かれた。屋根の上には、アイキャッチとして照明を内包した大きなアクリル製のキュービックなサインが設けられ、また、庇のデザインは、木組みの構造材や重厚な入り口扉と対比的に、薄く繊細なデザインとされた。ノスタルジックな外観に合わせ、内部は素材と色のコントラストによりシックで落ち着ける雰囲気に仕上げられた。

Coffee Club

Coffee Club is located in the suburbs of Takamatsu city on Shikoku island, in an area that continues to develop because of the completion of a road. This specialty shop targets coffee enthusiasts, so an individualistic architectural design was chosen to emphasize the building to its surroundings.

A stone wall facing the road and a gently rising stone staircase were built to clearly emphasize the building's existence. The exterior of the Coffee Club building is visible over the top of the wall.

Emphasis was placed on the designs of the roof and the eaves above the entrance. A large, cubic, internally lighted sign made of acrylic was installed on the roof to catch the eyes of passersby. The thin, delicate design of the eaves provides a contrast to the building's wooden framework and thick entrance door.

Inside the shop, the materials and colors contrast to creates a chic, calming atmosphere that complements the nostalgic exterior.

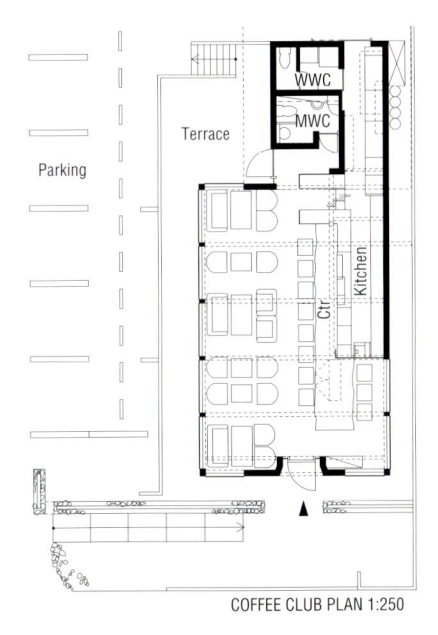

COFFEE CLUB PLAN 1:250

1. 道路とファサードの間に配された石塀と石の階段
2. パーキングスペースに面した奥の屋外テラス席
3. 入り口側から見た客席全景

1. A view of the facade from the street
2. A view of the terrace seating facing the parking area
3. A whole view of the interior from the entrance

ロケーションを生かしたオープンカフェ	Caffé MICHELANGELO

ミケランジェロ
東京・代官山

Sarugaku-cho, Tokyo
Designer: Kiyofumi Yusa
Photographer: Keisuke Miyamoto

設 計：R&Kパートナーズ
施 工：大作工務店　福田美装

1. 道路に迫り出したオープンカフェ客席
2. 奥のレストランと共有する中庭を店内から見る
3. 旧山の手通りに面したファサード。背後には2本のケヤキの大木が見える
4. 天井までガラス張りになった店内を左奥客席から見る

1. A view of the open seating facing the street
2. A view of the courtyard from the inside
3. A view of the facade through the Kyu-yamanote-doori
4. A view of the interior with a glass roof and glass walls

ガラスと鉄でできた開放的なつくり

閑静な高級住宅地におしゃれなショップが点在する東京・代官山、この地域を横断する幹線道路・旧山の手通りに面して「ミケランジェロ」はある。背後には60年前に建てられた古い洋館をレストランに改装した「ASO」があり、両者を隔てる中庭には樹齢200年のケヤキの大木が2本立っている。両者とも同じ会社が経営しており、カフェはレストランのエントランスとウエイティングの役割を果たしている。

周囲の恵まれた環境を生かして、イタリアのエスプリを感じてもらうのが店のコンセプトであり、そのため、全面ガラス張りの開放的なつくりとされた。ケヤキのある中庭は開放されており、夏場には本を読んで過ごしている人もいる。昼間の客層は年輩の女性客が多く、夕方は若い人やカップル、夜になるとグループ客がメーンとなる。

Michelangelo

Michelangelo faces the main thoroughfare Kyu-yama-note-doori in Daikanyama, Tokyo, a quiet, high-class residential district dotted with fashionable shops. The cafe shares a garden with the restaurant Aso, located behind it in a remodeled Western-style house built 60 years ago, and the garden is home to two 200-year-old Japanese zelkova trees. Michelangelo and Aso are managed by the same company, with the cafe serving as the restaurant's entrance and waiting area.

Taking advantage of its fortunate environment, Michelangelo was conceived as conveying Italian esprit, so it was given an open, all-glass design. The garden with the Japanese zelkovas is open to the public, and people can be seen reading books there in the summer. The cafe is patronized mainly by older women during the day, young people and couples in the evening and groups at night.

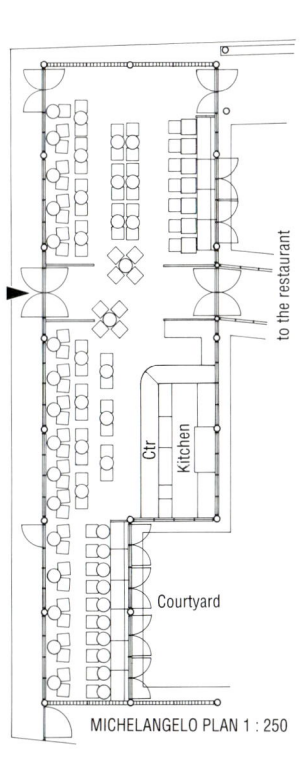

MICHELANGELO PLAN 1 : 250

| パリの老舗との提携で実現したオープンカフェ | Café de FLORE Omotesando |

カフェ・ド・フロール 表参道店

東京・神宮前

Jingumae, Tokyo
Designer: Yoshihisa Ichimura
Photographer: Hiro Photo

設計：エー・ピー・オー
施工：丹青社

パリのエレガンスとモダニズムを再現

パリを代表するカフェと提携した服飾雑貨メーカーが日本にオープンした二番目のカフェである。東京・原宿の元カフェバーを改装した店内は,道路に面した部分がオープンカフェ,トップライトのある奥部分がレストランとなっている。店づくりは,パリと同じメニュー,サービス,および雰囲気をそのまま再現することに主眼が置かれた。表参道に面したオープンカフェは,象牙色とゴールド,深紅と褐色の色彩のコンビネーション,東洋の伝統文様を思わせる床のモザイクタイル,フランスでリプロダクトされた照明器具などが時代を超え,モダンでエレガントな輝きを空間に与えている。階段状になったオープンカフェから,歩道とケヤキ並木をぼんやりと眺め,客はパリの気分をひととき体感できる。

Flore Omotesando

Flore Omotesando is the second cafe opened in Japan by a clothing and accessories manufacturer in partnership with a well-known Paris cafe. Inside this remodeled cafe and bar in Harajuku, Tokyo, an open cafe faces the street, and in the back is a restaurant with a skylight. The shop recreates the menu, service and atmosphere of the Paris cafe.

The open cafe facing Omotesando street uses a coloring scheme of ivory-white, gold, deep crimson and brown, along with mosaic floor tiling that recalls the traditional patterns of the Orient and lighting fixtures reproduced in France, to transcend its era and create a space that radiates modernity and elegance. Gazing at the sidewalk and a row of Japanese zelkova trees from the staircase-shaped open cafe, customers can momentarily experience the feel of Paris.

1. 店内奥客席から道路側オープンカフェ方向を見る
2. 開口部扉を開け放した状態のオープンカフェ客席
3. 開口部を閉じた状態のファサード夜景を表参道から見る
4. オープンカフェ側から見た奥のカフェ客席
5. 店内最奥部のレストラン客席

1. A view from the cafe to the open cafe
2. A night view of the open cafe
3. A night view of the facade from Omotesando
4. A view of the cafe from the open cafe side
5. A view of the restaurant behind the cafe

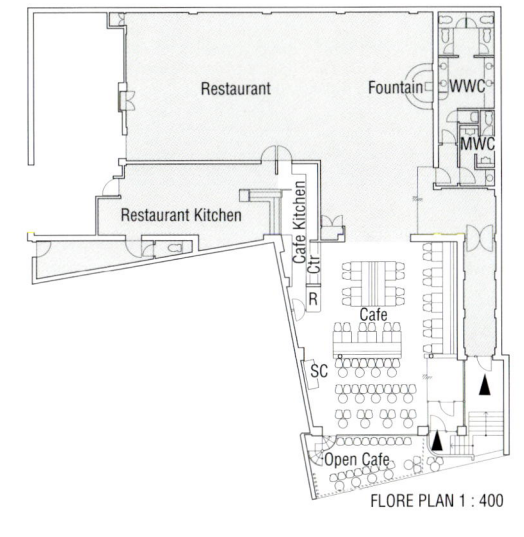

FLORE PLAN 1 : 400

都会の隠れ家的なエスプレッソカフェ

Espresso Cafe FORT McHENRY

フォート マックヘンリー

東京・恵比寿

Ebisu, Tokyo
Designer: Takamichi Kawakami
Photographer: Hikaru Suzuki

設計：ピーチプランニング
施工：ピーチプランニング

4

1. 入り口からアプローチ通路を通してカウンター方向を見る
2. カウンターバックに並ぶコーヒー豆のストック容器
3. カウンター前から入り口方向を見る
4. パーティションわきから見た奥客席とカウンター

1. A view from the entrance to the inner part
2. A view of the counter and coffee beans vessels
3. A view from the counter to the entrance
4. A view of the counter side seating from the partition

砦を象徴する素材としてのブリキ

東京・恵比寿のJR駅から徒歩1分のビル地下1階に「フォート マックヘンリー」はある。さまざまな種類のエスプレッソを提供するコーヒー専門店で、他に豆を煎るときに香り付けをしたフレーバーコーヒー、それにケーキやワッフルにも力を入れている。夜にはビールやワインなどのアルコール類も出す。
地下1階という立地から明るく開放的なカフェではなく、都会の隠れ家、オアシス的な砦というイメージで店づくりは進められた。内部は砦の外壁の象徴としてブリキがアクセントとして使われ、RC打ち放しの天井と相まって粗削りな空間となっているが、そこに温かさをプラスするため、パイン材の床や家具、土壁が配された。

Fort McHenry

Fort McHenry is located on the first underground floor of a building a minute's walk from Japan Rail's Ebisu Station in Tokyo. This coffee specialty shop serves a variety of espresso drinks and flavored coffees, along with cakes and waffles. At night, it also serves, beer, wine and other alcoholic beverages.
Because it is located underground, it was recommended that the shop aim for the image of an urban hideaway or oasislike fortress, rather than that of an open cafe. Galvanized steel sheets were placed inside as accents symbolizing the outer wall of a fortress. These combine with the ceiling of fair-faced concrete to create a space with an unfinished feel. Pine flooring and furniture, along with a mud wall, were added to give the shop warmth.

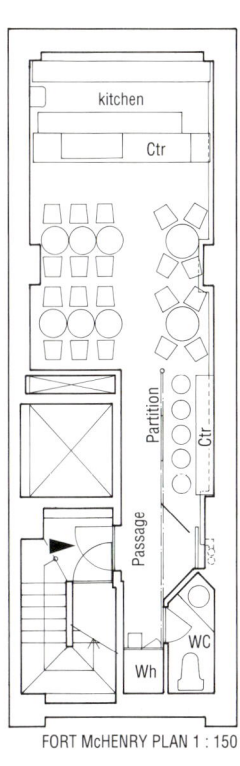

FORT McHENRY PLAN 1 : 150

"もてなしの場"としての自家焙煎珈琲店

鈴木
神奈川・厚木市

Coffee Shop SUZUKI

Naka-cho, Atsugi
Designer: Yukio Hashimoto
Photographer: Nacása & Partners

設 計： 橋本夕紀夫デザイン
　　　　スタジオ
施 工： 施工計画

1

1. 奥のコーヒーカウンター上に置かれたエスプレッソマシン側から入り口方向を見る
2. 腐食銅板を貼ったファサード夜景
3. 店内奥のコーヒーカウンター

1. A view from the coffee counter to the entrance
2. A night view of the facade with copper sheets
3. A view of the coffee counter

茶の湯の立礼スタイルを採り入れる

小田急線の東京と小田原市の中間に位置する厚木市。その駅前にあるビルの1階に「鈴木」は計画された。オーナーは近くの相模原市の店で、25年間コーヒーを煎れ続けてきた"こだわり"の人であり、今回の店に関しては、茶道のような"もてなし"でコーヒーを提供できる場をつくりたいというのがコンセプトであった。
店内は、茶道でイスに腰かけて茶を点てる立礼（りゅうれい）茶室にならい、中央に亭主（主催する人）が位置するカウンターが設けられ、その上に置かれた巨大なエスプレッソマシンからは蒸気が吹き出し、コーヒーが煎れられていく。間接照明による茶室のような暗めの空間の中で、客はオーナーが煎れてくれるコーヒーを落ち着いた気分で待ち、そしてコーヒーを飲みながら一刻を楽しむのである。

Suzuki

Atsugi is a city located between Tokyo and Odawara on the Odakyu train line. The coffee shop Suzuki was built on the first floor of a building in front of Atsugi Station. The owner, who ran a coffee shop in nearby Sagamihara city for 25 years and has definite opinions about coffee, conceived of Suzuki as a place to serve coffee in a manner similar to "sadou," or The Way of Tea.
The interior follows the example of a "ryurei" tearoom in which one sits on a sadou chair and makes tea. The owner operates an enormous, steaming espresso machine at a counter in the center of the shop. With indirect lighting used to maintain relative darkness like that in a tearoom, the customers can relax while waiting for the owner to make their coffee, and then enjoy the moment of drinking the finished product.

4. 間接照明を組み込んだ壁面ディテール
5. 入り口から見た店内全景

4. The detail view of the wall with indirect lighting
5. A whole view of the interior from the entrance

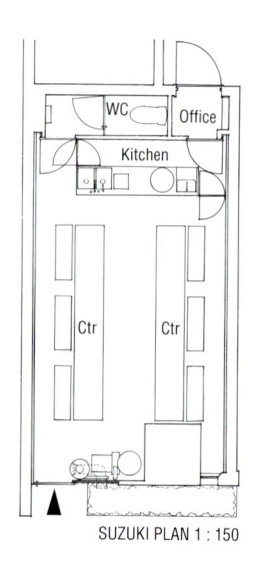

SUZUKI PLAN 1 : 150

やすらぎの空間を目指したピースフルなカフェ	Peaceful Cafe CHOPIN	
# ショパン 大阪・枚方市	Kawahara-cho, Hirakata Designer: Daisaku Takahashi Photographer: Seiryo Yamada	設 計：設計工房タカハシ 施 工：ライン企画

1

発光する2枚のスクリーン

大阪の郊外・枚方市の京阪線枚方市駅から徒歩3分のマンションビル1階に「ショパン」はできた。店づくりに関しては、ピースフルという店のネーミングから"やすらぎ"をイメージさせるデザインを、というのがクライアントからの要望であった。サイン類を最小に抑えた全面ガラス張りのファサードには、外部からの視線を遮りながら、内部の雰囲気を感じさせる高さに調節された2枚のスクリーンが取り付けられた。スクリーンの片面にはスチール板の表面に1列の小さな円形の穴が連続しており、そこから漏れる光がリズミカルなラインをつくりだしている。もう一つの面は布貼りのアクリル板で、照明が内側に埋め込まれているため前面が発光体となって光る。来客は布を通した淡い光と他の間接光とのコントラストを楽しみ、空間に"やすらぎ"を感じながら、時間を過ごすことができる。

Chopin

Chopin is located on the first floor of an apartment building three minutes by foot from the Hirakata city train station on the Keihan line in Hirakata, a suburb of Osaka. For the shop's design, the owner request a tranquil image in keeping with its peaceful name.

The signs in the all-glass facade were kept to a minimum, but the view from the exterior is obstructed by two screens tall enough to give just a hint of the atmosphere inside.

Light leaks through a series of small, round holes on the surface of the steel boards on one side of the screens, creating a rhythmical line. Lights placed on the inside of the cloth-covered acrylic boards on the other side of the screens causes them to radiate light.

Customers at Chopin experience a feeling of tranquility while enjoying the contrast between the pale light passing through the cloth and the other indirect lighting.

1. 入り口左側からライティングスクリーンとその奥のベンチシートを見る
2. 右奥の円形大テーブルから見た店内全景
3. 道路から見たファサード夜景。ライティングスクリーンが外部からの目隠しとなっている
4. 道路に面した楕円の大テーブル席を照らすライティングスクリーン

1. A view of the lighting screen and bench seating from the entrance
2. A whole view of the interior from the circular big table
3. A night view of the facade with lighting screen
4. A view of the oval big table surrounded with lighting screen

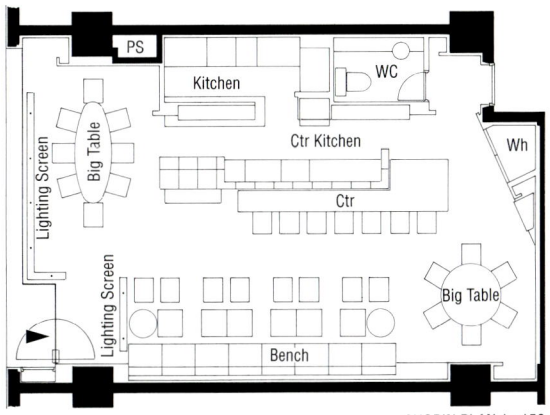

CHOPIN PLAN 1 : 150

京都駅ビルのにぎわう広場に面したカフェ

Cafe MUSICA LA LA

ムジカ・ラ・ラ

京都・烏丸通

Karasuma-doori, Kyoto
Designer: Satoshi Kusunoki
Photographer: Takeo Murase

設計：乃村工芸社
施工：乃村工芸社

1. 京都駅ビル7階の東広場に面した外観
2. 店内客席から東広場を見る
3. スキップアップしたテラスから見たファサード夜景
4. カウンター席から右奥方向の客席を見る

1. A view of the facade on the Kyoto station building seventh floor
2. A view from the inner seating to the outer plaza
3. A night view of the facade from the terrace floor level
4. A view of the seating from the counter side

シンプルでライトなデザイン

ホテル、デパート、専門店街などを包含した巨大なJR京都ステーションビルの内部に「ムジカ・ラ・ラ」はある。いろいろな催しが行われる7階の東広場に面しており、ビル内部でも人でにぎわう場所である。この立地条件を生かし、店舗としてのクオリティーを維持しながら、親しみやすく気軽に立ち寄れる店づくりが志向された。
間口が広く、奥行きのない店内はファサードがガラス張りなので、客席は外部からすべて見通せ、また、前面には屋外のテラス席が設けられている。奥の壁面を飾るイラストレーションはステーションビルをイメージしたもので、店内のシンプルでライトなデザインの空間の中で、人の手による温もりのある存在感を主張している。

Musica La La

Musica La La is located in the enormous Japan Rail Kyoto Station building, which is home to a hotel, department stores and collections of specialty shops. The cafe faces the 7th floor plaza, a particularly bustling spot that is the site of various events. The owner sought to take advantage of this prime location with a design that maintains the store's quality and is friendly and inviting.

The facade of Musica La La, a shop with a wide frontage but little depth, is made of glass, so the seating is all visible from outside. There is terrace seating in front of the shop. The illustrations on the walls inside are based on the station building, and they emphasize the warmth of human creation within this space of simple, light design.

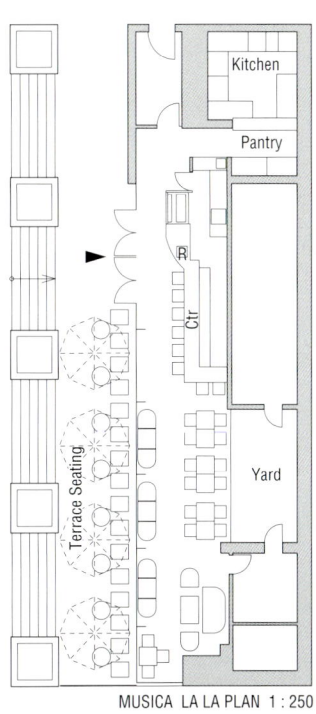

MUSICA LA LA PLAN 1:250

| シネマビルに併設されたアーティスト・カフェ | Cafe **CINEMA CAFE** |

シネマカフェ

東京・立川

Akebono-cho, Tachikawa
Designer: Haruki Kaito
Photographer: Nacása & Partners

設 計：海藤オフィス
施 工：乃村工芸社

アーティストの個性を前面に出した空間

映画館を中心とした複合商業ビル・シネマシティは、東京西部の郊外都市・立川のJR北口再開発地域に建てられた。このビル1階の4年間テナントが入居せず、空いたままのスペースに「シネマカフェ」は計画された。映画を見るための待ち時間、および見た後のひとときを過ごしてもらおうという意図である。

インテリアの特徴は、一人の前衛的なアーティストを前面に押し出し、店全体が彼のプライベートミュージアム的な空間とされていることである。壁面や柱、窓など、至るところに作品が飾られ、独特のコンテンポラリーな雰囲気をまき散らしている。客層は幅広いが、全体としては女性がやや多く、売り上げは映画館の売り上げと比例しているとのことである。

Cinema Cafe

Cinema City, a commercial complex centered on a movie theater, was built in a redeveloped area on the north side of the Japan Rail station in the western Tokyo suburb of Tachikawa. Cinema Cafe was opened on the first floor after it had remained vacant for four years without attracting any tenants. The cafe is intended as a place to pass the time before or after a movie. The interior is unusual in that it is a kind of private museum for a particular avant-garde artist. His works are found practically everywhere, adorning the walls, pillars and windows, and infusing the space with a contemporary atmosphere. Cinema Cafe has a broad customer base that includes slightly more women than men. The cafe's sales are proportionate to those of the theater.

1. ビル通路に面した奥のガラス壁面を利用したネズミのアートペイント
2. ビル内の開放的なファサード
3. 柱まわりを利用した大テーブル席から見たネズミのアートペイント壁面がある店内最奥客席
4. ネズミのアートペイントのある最奥客席から中央客席方向を見る
5. 入り口からアートの配された内部客席を見る

1. A view of the art painting "Rat" on the glass wall to the toilet
2. A view of the facade in the Cinema City building
3. A view of the seating beside the art painting "Rat"
4. A view from the art painting "Rat" to the center seating
5. A view of the center seating from the entrance

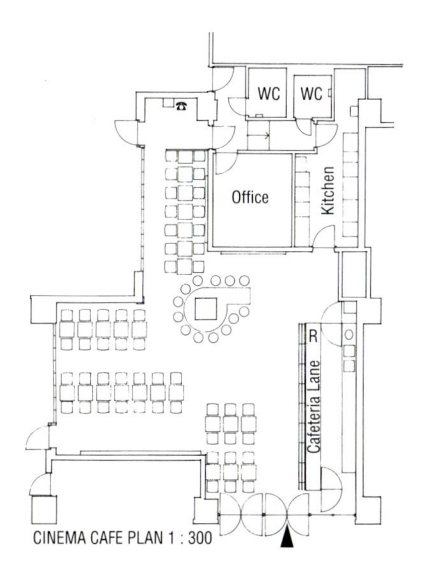

CINEMA CAFE PLAN 1 : 300

琵琶湖の眺望が楽しめるコーヒーショップ

Coffee Shop La Caffé KENYA

ラ カフェ ケニア

滋賀・大津市

Hama-machi, Ootsu
Designer: J.A.Laboratory
Photographer: Seiryo Yamada

設 計：ジェイ・エー・ラボラトリー
　　　 J.A.
施 工：八洋工芸

"心地よさ"をデザインする

滋賀県大津市の琵琶湖が眼前に見える場所にできたアミューズメントビル2階に「ケニア」はある。ファサードはビルのボードウオークに面し、正面に海のように広がる琵琶湖が望める。昼間は静かであるが、夜になると噴水とライトアップによるアトラクションを見ることができるという開放的で"心地よい"ロケーションをいかに生かすかが、店づくりのポイントとなった。

そこで、クールな印象のテラス席と、床・壁・天井がカバ桜材で覆われたウオームなテーブル席コーナーという趣の異なる二つの"心地よい"空間が設定された。さらに、快適な背もたれのついたイス、壁面がカーブして形作られたベンチシートによる"心地よい"座りの実現が追求され、他にもBGM、サービスなど、あらゆる店づくりの要素が心地よさを実現させる方向で決定された。

Kenya

Kenya is located on the second floor of an amusement building that commands a view of Lake Biwa in the city of Ootsu, Shiga Prefecture. The facade faces the building's boardwalk, and the oceanlike Lake Biwa is visible in front of the shop. An important point in Kenya's design was making the most of the open, comfortable location, which is quiet during the day, but at night draws crowds with attractions featuring bright lights and water fountains.

Two seating areas appealing to different tastes were set up in the shop. One has terrace seating and gives a cool impression. The other space has table seating and birch-plate-covered floors, ceilings and walls, and it gives an impression of warmth. The backed chairs and benches that curve in contour with the wall were designed, like the background music, service and every other element in the shop, to make customers comfortable.

1. アミューズメントビル2階に面したファサード夜景。前面には琵琶湖の眺望が広がる
2. 開口部に接したテラス席を入り口から見る
3. テラス席から見た奥客席。照明によって額縁のように浮き上がって見える
4. 人間の背のかたちに湾曲したカーブを持つベンチ席の壁面
5. 店内右奥客席から中央の大テーブル席方向を見る

1. A night view of the facade on the amusement building second floor
2. A view of the terrace seating from the entrance
3. A view of the inner part seating from the terrace area
4. A view of the bench seating with curved wall
5. A view from the right side bench seating to the big table

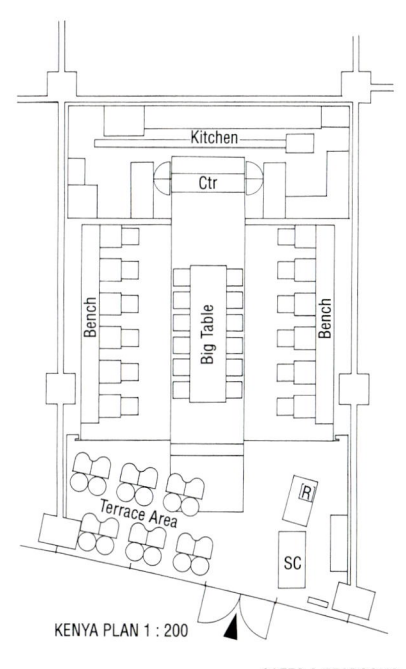

KENYA PLAN 1 : 200

新しいプロトタイプを目指すコーヒー専門店

シャノアール 両国店

東京・両国

Cafe CHAT NOIR Ryogoku

Ryogoku, Tokyo
Designer: Kazuhiro Nishino
Photographer: Shinichi Sato

設 計： 西野和宏
施 工： 日商インターライフ

公園をイメージした鉄製パーティション

現在、カフェの主流は、安くて美味しいコーヒーをセルフサービスで提供するコーヒー専門店であるが、旧来の喫茶店も店舗をリニューアルしたり、業態を変更して対応している。この「シャノアール両国店」は、従来から喫茶店のチェーン展開を行ってきた会社が、リニューアルのモデルケースとして全面的な改装を試みたものである。
デザイン的なテーマは"間仕切り"。それも一つ一つのブースを仕切るのではなく、大きく蛇行する連続した間仕切りによって空間全体を仕切り、デザイン的なポイントにすることが意図であった。スチールをクラフト的に加工した間仕切りは、向こう側が透けて見えるような意匠とされ、街路の延長線上にある公園のような雰囲気をつくりだしている。

Chat Noir Ryogoku

The current mainstream in cafes is self-service shops with inexpensive, delicious coffee, and many traditional cafes are remodeling and changing their business models to match this norm. A company developing a chain of coffee shops completely remodeled Chat Noir Ryogoku to serve as a model for its other shops.
The design theme is "partitioning." It refers not to partitioning the shop into separate booths, but to a large-scale partitioning of the entire space through a meandering series of continuous partitions. The crafted steel partitions were designed to leave the space on the other side visible, creating an atmosphere like that of a park above an extension of a road.

1. 厨房前の客席から円形パーティションに囲まれた客席を見る
2. レジ側から見た円形パーティション客席全景
3. 円形パーティション内側の客席
4. 入り口右側のベンチ席
5. ビル2階にある入り口まわり外観

1. A view of the seating surrounded with partition
2. A view of the seating from the cashier side
3. A view of the seating inside the partition
4. A view of the bench seating from the cashier side
5. A view of the entrance in the building

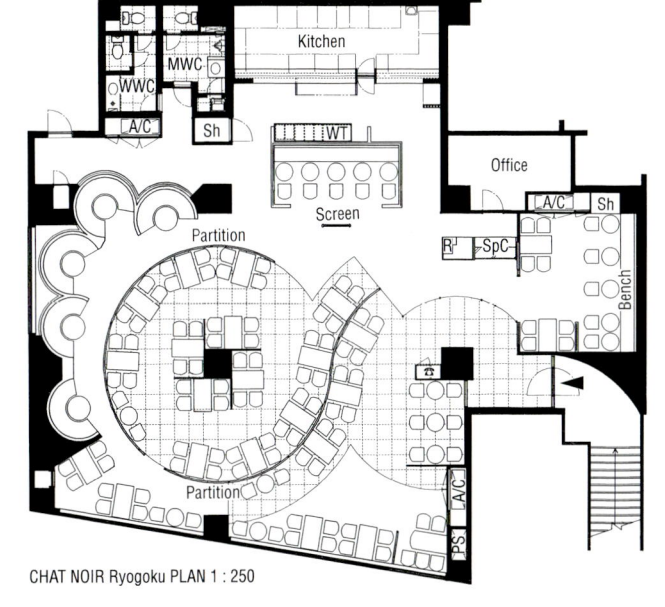

CHAT NOIR Ryogoku PLAN 1 : 250

本格的なエスプレッソを提供するデザートカフェ

Cafe CRESCENTE

クレシェンテ
東京・立川

Shibazaki-cho, Tachikawa
Designer: Hiroko Kubota
Photographer: Masaharu Nakatsuka

設 計：マッズプランニング
施 工：プラッツ

1. 通りから奥まった位置にあるファサード外観
2. 入り口から見た店内
3. 店内奥のベンチ席から厨房カウンター方向を見る
4. 奥客席中央に設けられた光りカウンターを厨房側から見る

1. A night view of the facade from the street
2. A view from the entrance to the inner part
3. A view from the bench seating to the kitchen side
4. A view of the lighting counter from the kitchen side

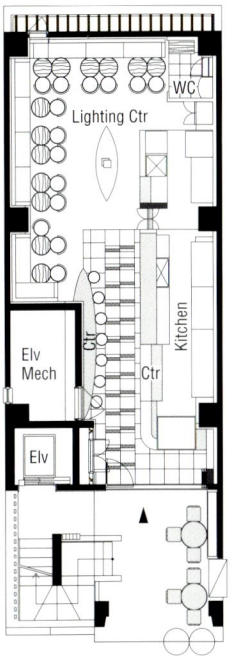

CRESCENTE PLAN 1:200

4

三日月をモチーフにした光りカウンター

東京西部に位置する郊外都市・立川のJR駅ビル斜め前にできた新築ビルの1階に「クレシェンテ」は計画された。本格的なエスプレッソとデザートを提供し、ファッショナブルでありながら気軽にゆったりとくつろげるという、新しいタイプのカフェをコンセプトに計画は進められた。

外観は、駅前の好立地であるが入り口が奥まった場所にあり、しかも間口が狭いという不利をカバーするため、道路から入り口に至る外壁にメニューやコーヒーカップなどをコラージュした大型の発光するアクリル製サインが取り付けられ、客導入が図られた。内部のデザイン的なシンボルとしては、奥客席中央に店名のクレシェンテ(三日月)をモチーフとしたアクリル製の光りカウンターが設けられ、カウンター上にも同じように発光するアクリル製のオブジェ照明が設置された。

Crescente

Crescente was built on the first floor of a new building that stands diagonally in front of the Japan Rail station building in the western Tokyo suburb of Tachikawa. It was conceived as a new type of cafe that offers authentic espresso and dessert, and is both fashionable and relaxing at the same time.

Despite its favorable location in front of a station, the shop is recessed within its building and has little frontage. To overcome these limitations, a large, lighted, acrylic sign decorated with a collage of the menu, coffee cups and other elements was installed on the external wall that runs from the road to the entrance.

A lighted, acrylic counter with a Crescente (crescent moon) motif was installed in the middle of the rear seating area to serve as a symbol. Glowing artistic objects made of the same acrylic material rest on the counter.

お洒落で美味しいカフェ＆ドルチェの店

ノア
東京・銀座

Caffé e Dolce **NOA**

Ginza, Tokyo
Designer: Hideki Shigeta
Photographer: Nacása & Partners

設 計：アクト
施 工：丹青社

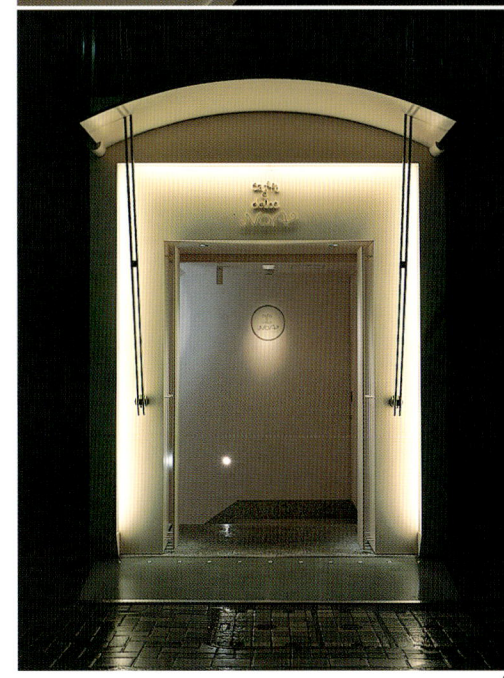

1. 客席Aの通路から見た奥のソファ席
2. レジから客席Bへの通路を見る
3. ビル1階に設けられた入り口ファサード
4. 1階から地下1階の店内へ至るアプローチ階段

1. A view of the sofa seating in the seating A
2. A view from the cashier to the seating B
3. A night view of the facade on the first floor
4. A view of the staircase from the first floor

太陽の光を演出したテラスとサロン

東京・銀座のビル地下1階にある「ノア」は20年以上前にオープンし、当時は店名の違う2軒の店として左右に分かれ、営業していた。今回の全面改装に際して、2軒の店を1店にすると同時に、時代に適応した業態への転身が図られた。どうせ、お茶を飲むなら、おしゃれな店で美味しいケーキと一緒に、という客層がターゲットである。
道路に面した1階入り口部分には、一戸建てのような庇を持つファサードが設けられ、そこから階段を下りて左右二つに分かれた客席に至る。客席の一つは少し落ち着いた感じのサロン的なイメージ、もう一つはフリーダムでテラス的なイメージとなっているが、全体的には優しく和らいだ色彩と雰囲気で統一されている。昼間の客層は30～50歳代の男性が60％、夜間は20歳代を中心とした女性客が90％を占め、客はその日の気分と目的によって、二つの客席を使い分けることができる。

Noa

Noa, located on the first underground floor of a building in Ginza, Tokyo, opened more than 20 years ago. At the time it was divided into two shops on the right and the left, each with a different name, but under common management. When the shops underwent a comprehensive remodeling, it was decided that they should be combined and their business model updated. Noa targets customers who prefer to drink their tea at a fashionable shop that also serves cake.
A facade with eaves like those on a detached house was installed in the entrance area facing the road on the first floor. A stairway leads down from there, splitting into right and left sections that lead to separate seating areas. One of the seating areas has a mellow, salonlike feel, and the other resembles a terrace and conveys a mood of freedom. The two sections are unified by a gentle, calming coloring scheme and atmosphere.
During the day, the customer base is 60 percent men between the ages of 30 and 50. At night, 90 percent of the customers are women, most in their 20s. At Noa, customers can choose their seating area according to their mood and purpose.

5. 客席Aの右奥コーナーから見た客席A全景
6. 客席Bをサービスステーション側から見る

5. A whole view of the seating A from the right corner
6. A view of the seating B from the service station

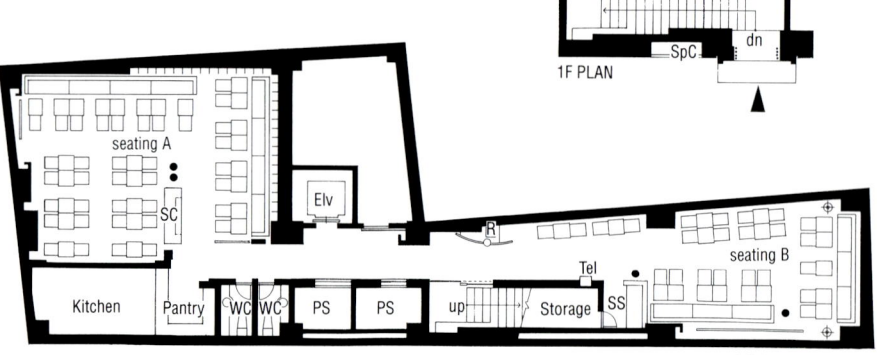

NOA B1 PLAN 1 : 250

| 新業態を併設したパイロットショップ | TAKANO Fruit Parlor & Fruit Bar |

タカノフルーツパーラー&フルーツバー
東京・新宿

Shinjuku, Tokyo
Designer: Keiji Nemoto
Photographer: Kaku Ootaki

設 計：根本恵司設計事務所
施 工：丹青社

1

1. 入り口エレベーターホールからアプローチゲートを通して店内を見る
2. フルーツパーラーの中央に配された花弁型の光り柱とそれを取り巻く座席
3. フルーツバーのバイキングカウンターを入り口側から見る

1. A view of the approach gate from the elevator hall
2. A view of the lighting pillar shaped like a flower in the fruit parlor
3. A view of the buffet-style fruit counter in the fruit bar

ガラス製の巨大な光る花がシンボル

東京・新宿のタカノといえば、長い歴史を持ち、東京に住む人ならば誰でも知っている有名な店舗である。本店2階にあるフルーツパーラーの延長として、業態をやや変化させながら三番目の店を新宿南口の商業ビル2階に出店した。バイキングスタイルのフルーツバーを入り口側に配し、奥に従来型のフルーツパーラーをジョイントした構成である。デザインのコンセプトはオーナーの要望で「レトロ」とされ、そのイメージに沿って時代感覚や感性が表現され、デザインされた。店内のシンボル的存在である花弁型の光り柱は網入りガラス製で、コンピューターの精度と計算力に職人の感性と経験がプラスされて実現した。フルーツパーラーの客層はヤングミセスが中心で、フルーツバーはやや年齢層の低い20歳代のOL、およびカップルが大部分を占める。

Takano

The fruit parlor and fruit bar Takano, located in Shinjuku, Tokyo, has a long history and is known by everyone in Tokyo. The third Takano outlet is located on the second floor of a commercial building on the south side of Shinjuku Station. It was opened as an annex to the main location's second-floor fruit parlor, but has a slightly different business model. There is a buffet-style fruit bar next to the entrance that is run jointly with a traditional fruit parlor in the back.
At the owner's request, the designer adopted a retro theme for the interior. A lighting pillar shaped like a flower serves as a symbol of the shop. This wire-glass fixture is the product of a computer's accuracy and calculation power and a craftsman's sensitivity and experience. The fruit parlor's customers are mainly young, married women. The fruit bar attracts mainly female office workers in their 20s and couples.

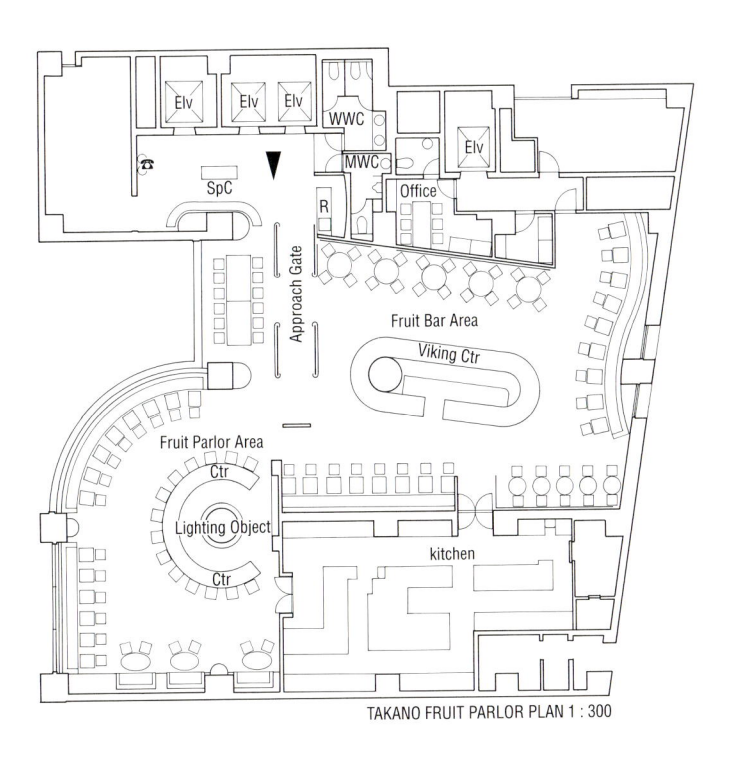

TAKANO FRUIT PARLOR PLAN 1 : 300

ヤング対象のヘルスコンシャスなカフェ

Cafe **JUICE PLUS**

ジュースプラス

東京・新宿

Shinjuku, Tokyo
Designer: Tadayuki Miyogawa
Photographer: Keisuke Miyamoto

設 計：A＆I
施 工：伊勢丹

1

'60～'70年代のSF的テイストを表現

以前はティールームであった東京・新宿のデパートの一角が改装され、ヘルスコンシャスなカフェへと業態が変更された。「ジュースプラス」とネーミングされた店のテーマは"美と健康"であり、"ファッショナブルな実験室"が目指された。従来の飲食店では医療的なイメージはタブーであったが、近年のサプリメント・ブームや複合機能食品のヒットなどにより常識が変化しつつある。その流れを捉え、複合機能を全面に押し出して先鋭的な顧客層の支持を得ることが目的であった。

店内のデザインは、いまだテクノロジーが夢を見ていた「'60～'70年代のSF的テースト」がメーンコンセプトとされ、明るく真っ白な空間に装飾としてアクリル樹脂が多用された。客層は20代前半のヤングが80％を占めるが、インテリアに惹かれた子供連れや外国人の利用もしばしば見られる。

Juice Plus

A tearoom in a corner of a Shinjuku, Tokyo, department store was remodeled and made into a health-conscious cafe. Named Juice Plus, the shop was given the theme of "beauty and health." Its owner intended it to be a "fashionable laboratory." A medicinal image used to be taboo for conventional eating and drinking establishments. But in recent years, the supplement boom and a string of hit foods boasting multiple health benefits have caused sensibilities to change. The owner noticed this trend and formed the goal of attracting sharp customers with an appetite for these "composite" foods.

The main interior design concept of the shop is the science fiction of the '60s and '70s, when today's technology was still a dream. Abundant use was made of polymethyl methacrylate to decorate the bright, white space. Eighty percent of Juice Plus' customers are in their early 20s, but families whose children are drawn to the interior and non-Japanese customers are also frequently seen in the cafe.

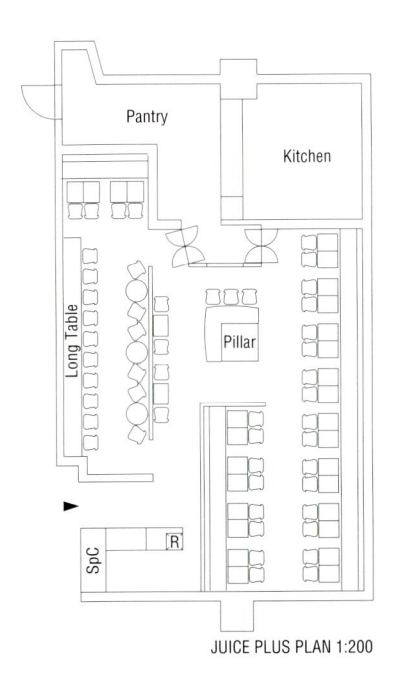

JUICE PLUS PLAN 1:200

1. レジ側から見た左側客席のロングカウンター席
2. デパート通路から見た入り口まわり外観
3. 右側客席から厨房方向を見る

1. A view of the long counter seating from the cashier side
2. A view of the entrance from the department store passage
3. A view from the bench seating to the kitchen side

チェーン展開を目指す手作りベーグル・カフェ

Bagel Shop e-STREET BAGELS Toranomon

e-ストリート ベーグルズ 虎ノ門

東京・西新橋

Nishi-shinbashi, Tokyo
Designer: Hiroyuki Tsujinaka
Photographer: Kaku Ootaki

設 計：ワックストラックス
施 工：貴プランニング

1

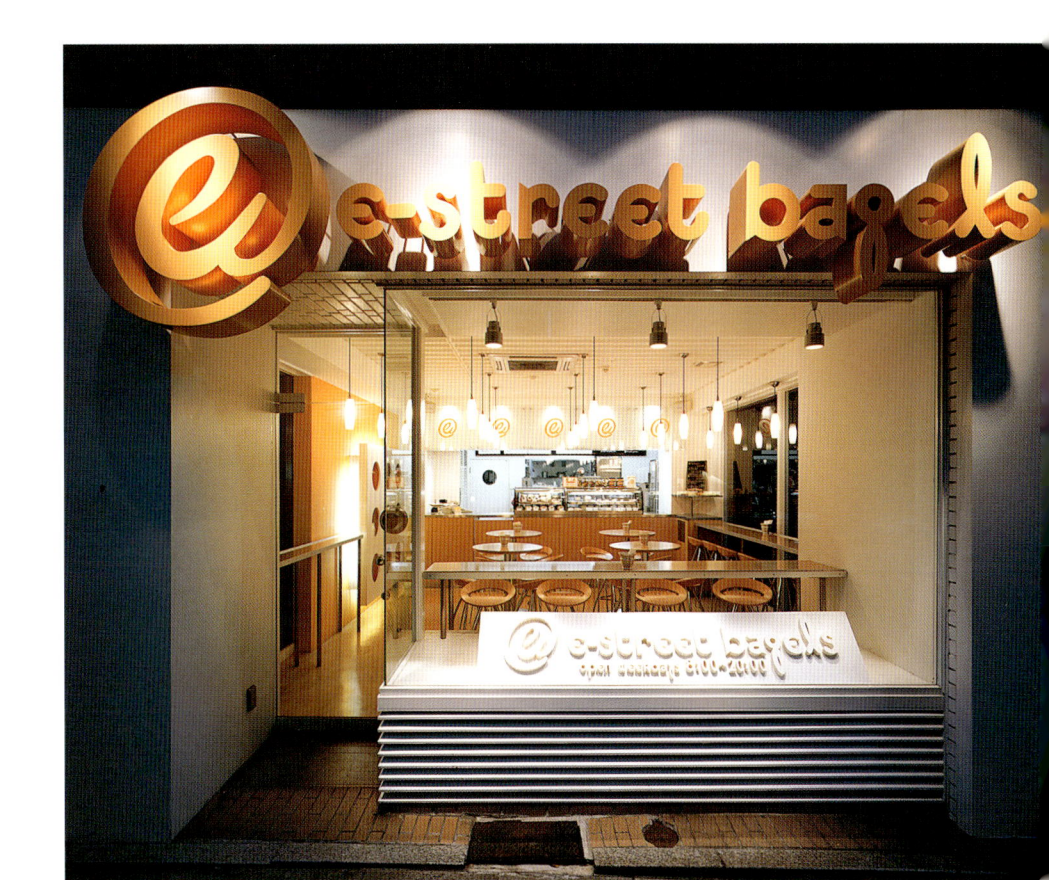

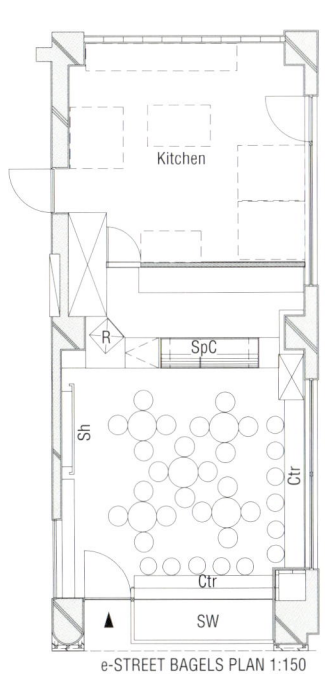

ブランドイメージのためのロゴと色彩

アメリカに長く住んでいたオーナーが、日本にも美味しいベーグルの店が欲しいと企画したのが、東京・西新橋にできた「e-ストリート ベーグルズ」である。フランチャイズ展開によるチェーン化を前提に、ショップアイデンティティーを確立し、ブランドイメージを形成するための店づくりが進められた。

店づくりのコンセプトとしては、情報化社会の最小の記号単位である@=アットマークがモチーフとして採用され、イメージカラーのイエローで統一された空間に@のグラフィックが配された。店舗機能は、ファストフードレストランのセオリーに則した効率的なレイアウトが重視され、それ以外の要素は最小限にとどめられている。

e-Street Bagels

Having lived in the United States for a long time, the owner of e-Street Bagels in Nishi-Shinbashi, Tokyo, opened the shop because he wanted there to be a place in Japan that serves delicious bagels. He was encouraged to adopt a design that would establish his shop's identity and brand image before he branched out into a franchise chain.

A design motif of the @ symbol - the smallest symbol of the information age - was adopted, and the character was distributed throughout the all-yellow interior.

For functionality, an efficient layout that conforms to fast-food theory was emphasized. Unnecessary elements were kept to a minimum.

e-STREET BAGELS PLAN 1:150

1. 店内右側カウンター席から左側壁面のディスプレイ棚方向を見る
2. 道路から見たファサード夜景

1. A view from the counter seating to the wall display shelves
2. A night view of the facade from the street

CAFES & TEAROOMS 99

3業態を同時併存させた三毛作デリカフェ

Deli-cafe REGARO Toranomon

レガーロ 虎ノ門店
東京・虎ノ門

Toranomon, Tokyo
Designer: Takashi Shimizu
Photographer: Masaharu Nakatsuka

設計：ドス・パートナーシップ
施工：三平リフォーム

オープンキッチンで空間全体を演出

東京・虎ノ門のオフィス街にあるビル1階に「レガーロ」はある。新橋に続く第2店目であり、一つの店に三つの業態を持たせた"三毛作"店である。奥に細長い店内は、フロントゾーンがコンビニ的な要素を備え、グロッサリーを中心とした販売ゾーン、ミッドゾーンが、冷蔵ショーケースから客が選んだフライをその場で揚げ、パンに挟んで提供するデリカフェ、最奥部がレストランゾーンという構成。

従来の"三毛作"店は、照明の明るさにより雰囲気を変えたり、カウンターのバック棚を移動させたりして、同じ空間を時間によって使い分ける手法を採っていた。しかし、この店の場合は、中央にオープンキッチンを置くことで調理をしている様子をストレートに見せ、シズル感を演出して空間をワンイメージにすることにより、一つのスペースの中に同時"三毛作"の店舗をつくりだしている。

Regaro Toranomon

Regaro is located on the first floor of a building in an office section of Toranomon, Tokyo. It is a three-in-one establishment that is the second in its chain, having been built after the Shinbashi outlet. Inside the long, narrow shop, one first finds the front zone, which is like a convenience store and mainly sells groceries. Next is the middle zone, which is a deli cafe full of refrigerated showcases from which customers choose ingredients that are deep-fried on the spot and made into sandwiches. Finally, in the back, is the restaurant zone.

Three-in-one shops usually transform themselves at different times of day by, for example, adjusting the lighting to change the atmosphere and moving the shelving located behind the counter. Regaro, however, is able to be three different businesses at the same time. It achieves this through an open kitchen placed in its center that allows customers to watch the cooking. The sight, sound and smell of sizzling food unify the space with a common theme.

1. レジから奥のレストラン客席方向を見る
2. 店内中央のオープン厨房とカウンター席
3. 入り口右側面のビル通路から見た
   デリのイートイン客席
4. 道路から見たファサード夜景
5. 店内最奥部のレストランソファ席

1. A view from the cashier to the inner part
2. A view of the open kitchen and counter seating in the center
3. A view of the eat-in deli seating from the outside
4. A night view of the facade from the street
5. A view of the inner part restaurant seating

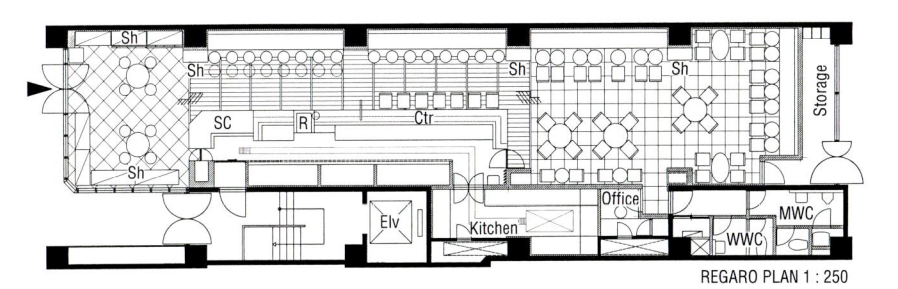

REGARO PLAN 1 : 250

買い物客の主婦が対象のティールーム

グリーン
東京・南麻布

Tearoom GREEN

Minami-azabu, Tokyo
Designer: Kenichi Kamiyama
Photographer: Osamu Tomita

設 計：U/A
施 工：プロシード

グリーンを引き立てる純白の空間

東京・広尾は、各国の大使館が点在し、都心部にありながら閑静な雰囲気の高級住宅地である。白の外観を持つ商業ビル・広尾ガーデンは地下鉄広尾駅の前にあり、「グリーン」はその2階に位置する。メーンの客層は待ち合わせや、ビルへ買い物にきた女性客である。

改装に際しては、このような街のイメージと周囲のロケーションがデザインに反映された。ビル通路との境界を仕切ってない開放的な空間は、床・壁・天井が純白のカラーに統一され、テーマカラーのグリーンを引き立てるステージの役割を果たしている。店内の中央にはトップライトからの自然光が降り注ぐ植物のプランターが吊り下げられ、壁面には流れる水の壁画が描かれた。また、ベンチ席両側の壁にはミラー貼りのストライプが設けられ、店内の表情を断片的に映し出している。

Green

Hiroo, Tokyo, an area dotted with embassies, is a high-grade residential area with a quiet atmosphere, despite its location in the city center. The tearoom Green is located on the second floor of Hiroo Garden, a commercial building with a white exterior that stands in front of the Hiroo subway station. Green's customers are primarily young women who come to wait for friends or shop in the building.

When the tearoom was remodeled, the surroundings and the image of the neighborhood were incorporated into the design. The floor, walls and ceiling of Green's open interior, which is not partitioned off from the building's passageway, are pure white. This white acts as a stage on which to display the tearoom's signature color: green.

Planters hang from the ceiling, in the center of which is a skylight. A mural depicting flowing water decorates the walls. Mirrored stripes on the walls on either side of the bench seating produce layers of reflections of the interior faces.

1. 奥客席の天井トップライト下部に吊り下げられたグリーン
2. ビル通路から見た入り口わきのカウンター席と厨房
3. 壁面のストライプに貼られたミラーに映り込んだ店内

1. A view of the plant pots under the skylight
2. A view of the counter seating and kitchen from the building passage
3. A view of the stripe mirror on the wall

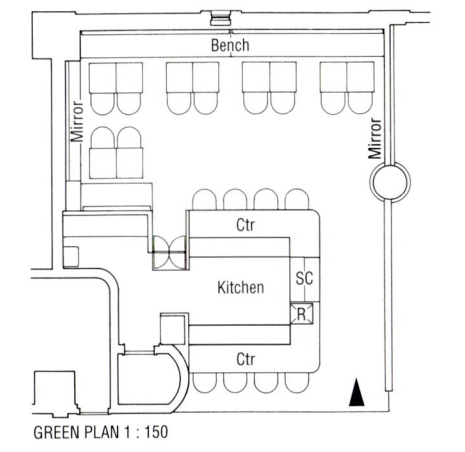

GREEN PLAN 1:150

近隣の女性を対象にした住宅街の甘味喫茶 | Japanese Cafe Arashiyama UJIAN

嵐山 宇治庵

千葉・おゆみ野

Oyumino-cho, Chiba
Designer: Yasuaki Ryu
Photographer: Nacása & Partners

設計：ティー・ワイ・デザイン
施工：店舗研究室

1. 道から見たファサード夕景。外壁表面はタペストリー加工のアクリル板
2. レジ背後の客席から中央大テーブル席方向を見る
3. 入り口外部に突き出したかたちの中央大テーブル
4. 入り口側から見た大テーブル。ガラストップの下には人工グリーンが配されている

1. An evening view of the facade from the street
2. A view from the right side seating to the center big table
3. A view of the big table from the entrance
4. A view from the big table to the inner part wall

昔の京都の町並みを再現した内部空間

東京の近郊・千葉市の住宅地にできた「嵐山 宇治庵」は、特徴のあるファサードを持っている。青空をイメージさせる、白とブルーのパターンに塗り分けられた外壁の上に、すりガラスのような風合いを持ったアクリル板を重ね、水墨画のような"にじみ"効果を表現している。

「昔の京都のような町並みを感じながら、戸外で食べているイメージ」というオーナーの要望により、なされたデザインであり、内部もこのコンセプトに沿ってデザインが展開された。店内は庭、軒下、家の中という三つの要素で構成され、これらを一つの空間に凝縮することで、古都の町並みや庭の雰囲気が感じられるよう意図された。また、中央には金沢の兼六園にある緑の中の茶室をイメージした、人工グリーンを下部に配した透明ガラス製の大テーブルが置かれている。

Arashiyama Ujian

The cafe Arashiyama Ujian, located in a residential area in the Tokyo suburb of Chiba city, has a distinctive facade. Acrylic boards with the texture of ground glass have been affixed to an external wall, which is painted alternately white and blue to suggest the blue sky. The effect resembles the runny ink of an India-ink painting.

The shop's design was based on the owner's desire to convey "the image of eating outdoors while experiencing an old-time Kyoto street of shops and houses." The interior is composed of three conceptual elements: a garden, the overhang of a Japanese roof and the inside of a Japanese house. The designer condensed these elements into one space to communicate the atmosphere of a garden and street of shops and houses in the former capital. Large tables of transparent glass with embedded green grass sit in the middle of Arashiyama Ujian. They are based on the image of a tearoom that is located amid the greenery of the garden Kenrokuen in Kanazawa.

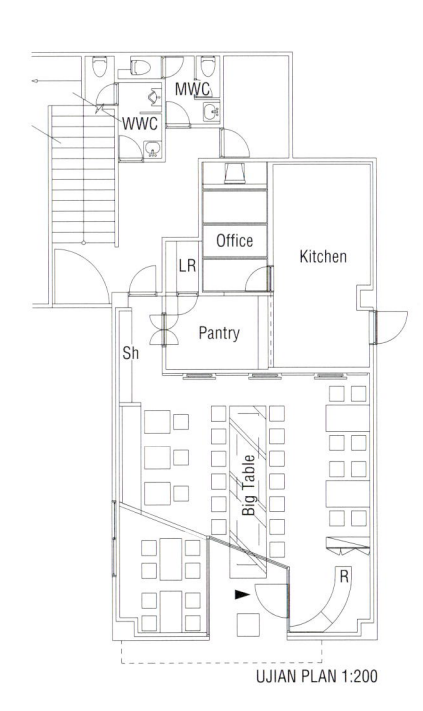

UJIAN PLAN 1:200

中国茶を中心としたティールーム	Chinese Tearoom **CHA YŪ**	
茶語 東京・北青山	Kita-aoyama, Tokyo Designer: Koji Nonogami Photographer: Keisuke Miyamoto	設 計：ジアス・アソシエイツ 施 工：ゼニヤ東京支店

独自のミニマムシックなスタイルを構築

東京・青山にあるファッションビル・青山ベルコモンズの5階にできた「茶語」は、各種の茶の卸しをしている会社が経営しており、新宿に続き第2店目となる。店づくりのコンセプトは、1店目と同じく「茶語的ミニマムシックスタイルの創造」。シンプルな空間に爽やかな「風」と柔らかい「光」のリズム感を感じさせることで、心地よい安らぎをつくりだすことに主眼が置かれた。
入り口まわりに配されたモルタル壁面には中国茶の名前が彫り込まれて、中国的な雰囲気とダイナミックな環境が表現された。また、高い天井を生かした縦の格子壁は、透けて見える外部の光と影のコントラストを、静けさの中に感じさせる。

Cha Yū

Cha Yū, located on the fifth floor of a fashion building called Aoyama Bellcommons in Aoyama, Tokyo, is managed by a company that wholesales various types of tea. It is the second shop in its chain, having been built after a Shinjuku outlet. The design concept is the same as that of the Shinjuku store: minimalist chic. It emphasizes suggesting the rhythms of gentle light and a refreshing breeze within a simple, relaxing space.
The names of Chinese teas are engraved on the mortar walls around the entrance, creating Chinese atmosphere and dynamic environment. Taking advantage of the high ceiling, tall, latticed wooden walls were used. Light from outside can be seen through these walls, and it contrasts with the shadows in this quiet space.

1. ビル通路側入り口から見たレジまわり
2. レジ前からウエイティングエリア方向を見る
3. ルーム-1の右奥コーナー客席とディスプレイ棚
4. レジ前からディスプレイ棚の間を通してルーム-1方向を見る
5. ビル通路側から見たルーム-2

1. A view of the cashier from the building passage side entrance
2. A view from the building side entrance to the waiting area
3. A view of the inner part seating in the room-1
4. A view from the cashier side to the room-1
5. A view of the room-2 from the building passage side entrance

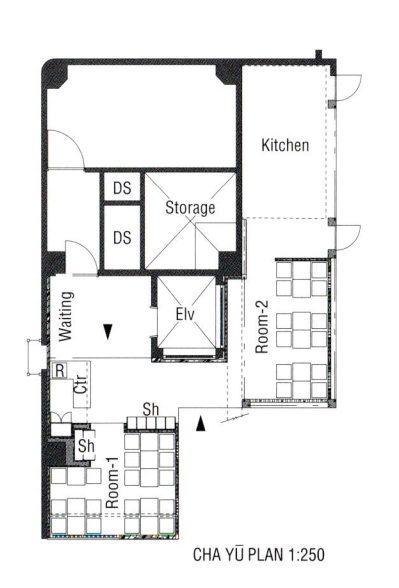

CHA YŪ PLAN 1:250

庭園に面した茶道会館内部のティーラウンジ

Tearoom **LOUNGE 235**

ラウンジ 235
京都・六角通り

Rokkaku-doori, Kyoto
Designer: Tatsuhiko Ito
Photographer: Hiroshi Fujiwara

設 計：カジマデザイン
施 工：鹿島

1

1. スロープから奥のソファ席方向を見る
2. エレベーターホール側から見た客席全景
3. 客席からキッチン方向へアプローチ通路を見る

1. A view from the approach slope to the sofa seating
2. A whole view of the seating from the elevator hall
3. A view of the approach passage from the inner part

曲面と間接照明による柔らかなイメージ

華道で最古の伝統を誇る池坊の、京都にある本拠地のビル1階に設けられたティールーム。華道の先生たちや本部スタッフの憩いの場、語らいの場としてつくられた。

本館の東側に増築された部分の1、2階を吹き抜けとし、大きなガラス面の開口部を通して素晴らしい眺めの池と庭園に接している。

卵形の平面形状と断面を持つラウンジのインテリアは、曲面を多用した柔らかなイメージの空間であり、高いドーム天井と間接照明によって、その効果がよりいっそう強調されている。

世界から集められた1,124種類のスプーンを飾ってある壁面を背に、見る角度により和にも洋にもイメージを変える庭園を見ながら、全国から集まった華道の先生たちは互いに楽しく語らい、情報交換の時間を過ごすことができる。

Lounge 235

The tea room Lounge 235 is located in Kyoto on the first floor of the Ikenobo Headquarters Building, an international center for "ikenobo," the oldest flower arrangement tradition in Japan. Lounge 235 was created as a place for flower arrangement teachers and headquarters staff to rest and chat. The first and second floors of an addition to the east of the main building make up a well that contains Lounge 235 and a large, glass-covered aperture, through which can be seen a beautiful pond and garden. The tea room's interior contains egg-shaped planes and cross sections, and it uses many curved surfaces to create a soft image. The effect of softness is reinforced by a high, domed ceiling and indirect lighting. One wall in the tea room is decorated with a collection of 1,124 spoons from various nations. With this collection in the background, flower arrangement instructors from around the world chat and exchange information here, while viewing the garden, which appears either Western or Japanese, depending on the viewing angle.

4. 池のある庭園に面した開口部側客席
5. 外部の庭園から見た外観夜景

4. A view of the seating facing the garden and pond
5. A night view of the facade from the garden

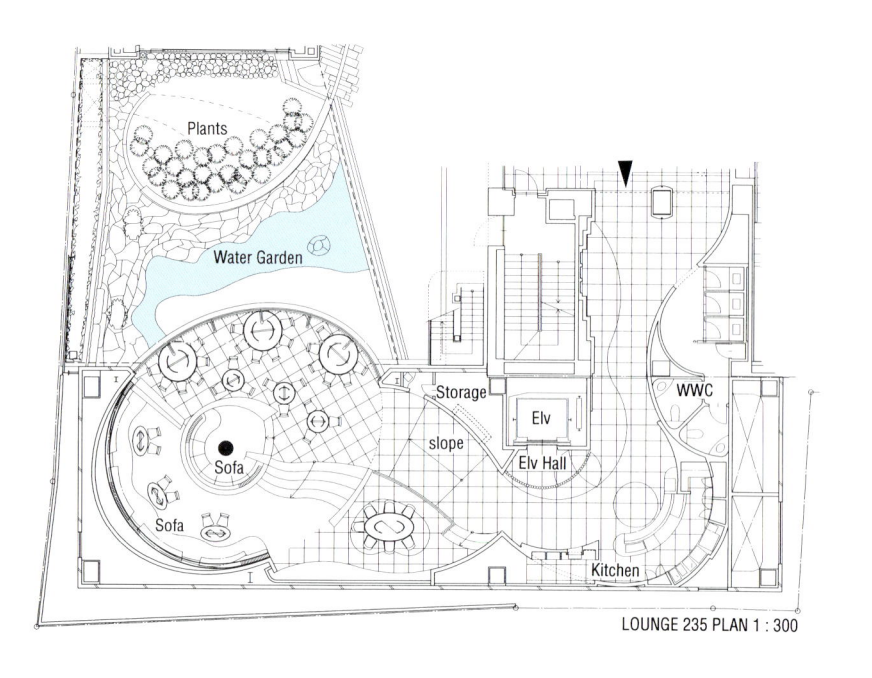

LOUNGE 235 PLAN 1 : 300

SHOP DESIGN SERIES
CHAPTER 3

CAFE-
RESTAURANTS

| トラットリアをイメージした多目的ダイニングカフェ | Dining-cafe **RICORDI** |

リコルディ
京都・縄手通

Nawate-doori, Kyoto
Designer: Hisanobu Tsujimura
Photographer: Nacása & Partners

設 計： 辻村久信デザイン事務所
施 工： 正棟建築工業

1

1. 奥の映写スクリーン側から入り口方向全景を見る
2. アプローチ通路からパーティション円形開口部を通して見たバーカウンター
3. エレベーターホールから見た入り口アプローチ通路

1. A whole view of the interior from the screen side
2. A view of the bar counter from the partition hole
3. A view of the approach passage from the elevator hall side

オパール色に包まれた照明空間

古都・京都で800年以上の歴史を持ち、格式を誇る色町・祇園にできた「リコルディ」は、周囲の伝統的な町並みとは対照的なインテリアを持ったカフェ・レストランである。カラオケ店などを経営するオーナーがイタリア好きで、イタリアの本格的なトラットリアをイメージしてつくられた。
店内は、低い天井をカバーするため照明は床と壁に埋め込まれ、その結果、空間全体に光がまわり、影のない不思議な雰囲気に包まれることとなった。特に床に埋め込まれた光源のカバーに使われているオパールガラスは黄緑色をしており、そこを透過した光は白い壁と天井を黄緑色に染め上げている。また、将来はイベントやアートの展覧会、映画の上映などができるように、奥の壁面にはスクリーンが取り付けられ、テーブルやイスも簡単に移動できるようになっている。

Ricordi

Ricordi is a cafe-restaurant located in the prestigious, more than 800-year-old pleasure quarter of Gion in the former capital of Kyoto. Its interior provides a contrast to the surrounding, traditional streets of houses and shops. The owner, who also runs karaoke establishments, is an Italophile, and he created Ricordi in the image of an authentic trattoria.
Because the shop has a low ceiling, lights were embedded in the floor and walls. The resulting light fills the space, creating a curious atmosphere characterized by a lack of shadows. The lights embedded in the floor are covered with yellowish-green opal glass, and they bathe the white walls and ceiling in the same color.
For possible future events such as art exhibits and film screenings, a screen was installed on the back wall and the interior was arranged so that the tables and chairs can easily be moved.

4. レジ側からバーカウンターを通して奥方向を見る
5. シネマを上映できる状態に家具を片づけたテーブル席。奥壁面には映写用のスクリーンが収納されている

4. A view from the cashier side to the inner part
5. A view from the DJ booth to the inmost wall for film screenings

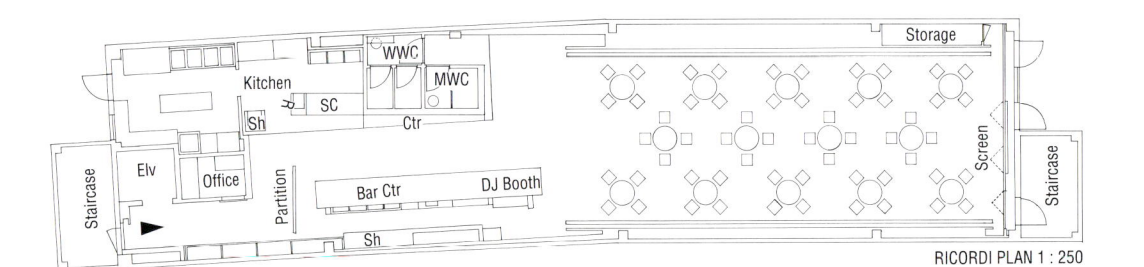

RICORDI PLAN 1 : 250

1階をオープンキッチンにしたカフェレストラン

Cafe-restaurant LOTUS

ロータス
東京・神宮前

Jingumae, Tokyo
Designer: Ichiro Katami
Photographer: Nacása & Partners

設 計： 形見プランニングサービス
施 工： ディーブレーン

シンボリックな光る壁の蓮の花

東京でも指折りのファッショナブルな街・原宿にできた「ロータス」は、ビルの1階と地下1階を占めている。1階の大部分はオープンキッチンであり、メーンの客席は地下にある。自らも飲食店を経営し、また、飲食店のプランナーでもあるオーナーからは、時代や流行に消費されないで永く残るデザインが要望された。

店づくりに際しては、間口が狭く奥行きのある平面形状のなかで、いかに地下へ客を誘導するかが検討され、店内の奥、オープンキッチンの後ろ側に階段が設けられた。そこまで来客を引き寄せるため、最奥部分に1階と地下1階をつなぐ吹き抜け空間が設けられた。また、地下1階の道路側壁面には照明を裏側に埋め込んだアクリル製の光り壁が配されており、表面に取り付けられた巨大な蓮の花の写真は、背後からの光りを通して発光体となり、この店のシンボルともなっている。

Lotus

The cafe-restaurant Lotus occupies the first floor and first underground floor of a building in Harajuku, a particularly fashionable part of Tokyo. An open kitchen takes up most of the first floor, and the main customer seating area is underground. The owner, who manages the shop himself and is a planner of food-and-drink establishments, sought a design that would never go out of style.

After considering how to guide customers through the long, narrow shop to the underground seating, the owner installed a staircase behind the open kitchen. The wall closest to the street on the first underground floor is made of acrylic and has embedded back lights. It is decorated with an enormous photograph of lotus flowers through which the light passes. This glowing photograph serves as a symbol of the shop.

1. 道路側から見た外観夕景
2. 1階から階段を通して地下1階を見る
3. 店奥の吹き抜けに面した客席
4. 地下1階のダムウエイターわきから階段方向を見る
5. 地下1階の階段わきからライティングウオール方向を見る
6. 蓮の花が表面をおおう地下1階のライティングウオール

1. An evening view of the facade
2. A down view of the first basement floor through the staircase
3. A view of the inmost seating on the first floor
4. A view from the dumb waiter to the staircase on the first basement floor
5. A view from the staircase to the lighting wall on the first basement floor
6. A view of the lighting wall on the first basement floor

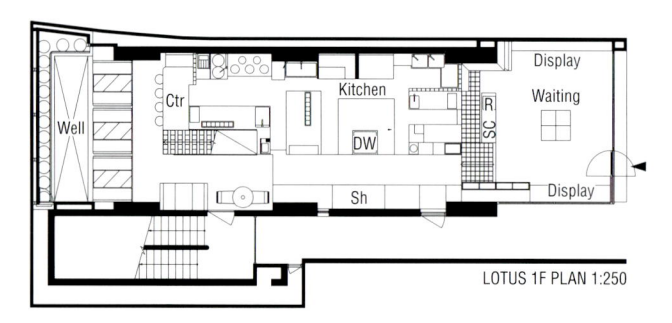

LOTUS 1F PLAN 1:250

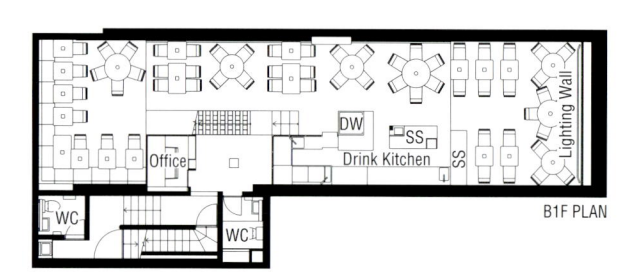

B1F PLAN

CAFE-RESTAURANTS 117

木造倉庫をリニューアルしたカフェレストラン

Cafe-restaurant **CHARBON**

シャルボン

大阪・北堀江

Kita-horie, Osaka
Designer: Toshiharu Minami
Photographer: Seiryo Yamada

設 計：スタジオ ソフィア
施 工：英進

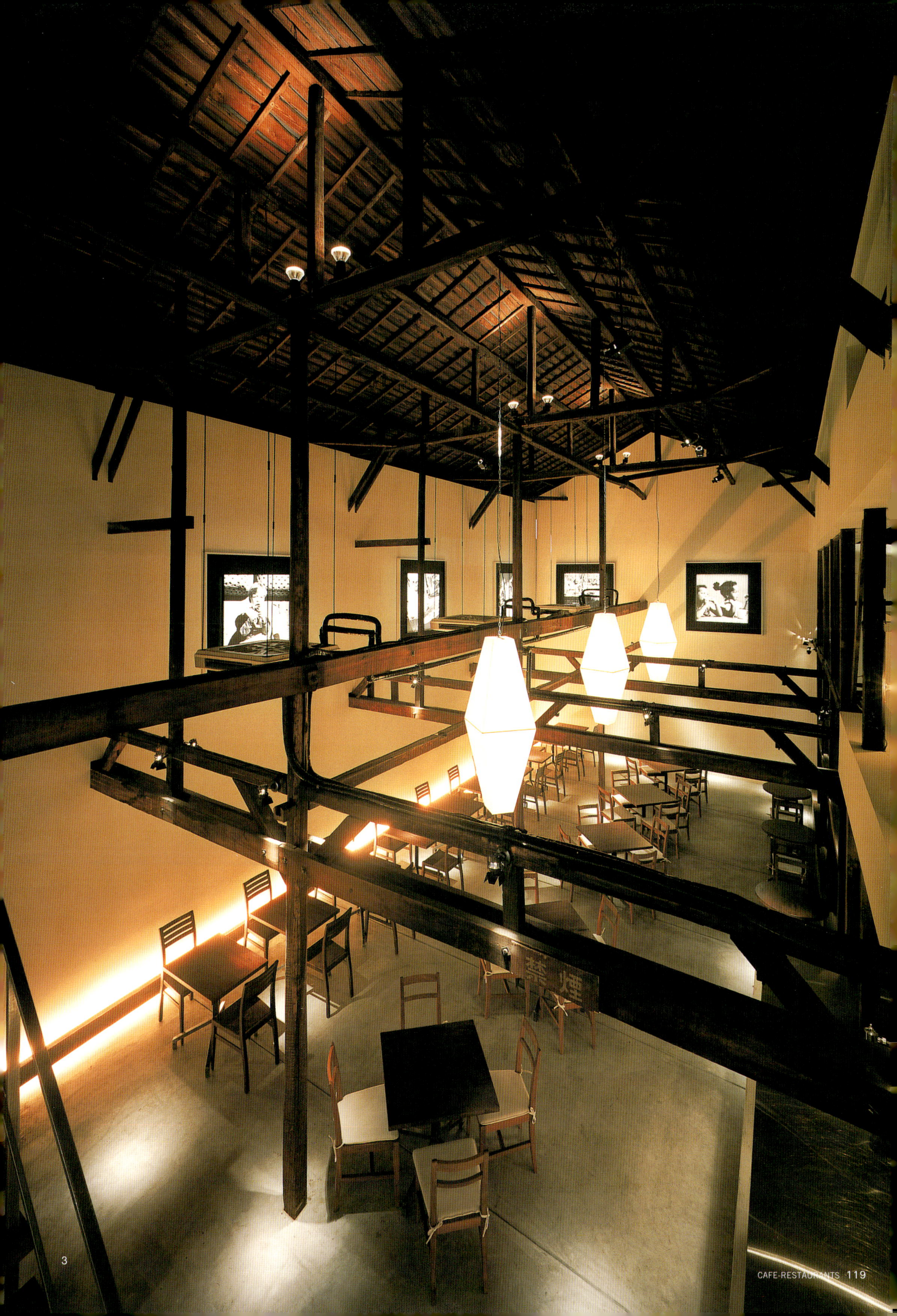

3

倉庫の大空間と時代の空気を残す

大阪のファッショナブルな若者たちが集まる"アメリカ村"。その西に位置する北堀江にも、昔ながらの商店街の中に新しい感覚のショップができ始めた。「シャルボン」は北堀江の一角にある木造2階建ての倉庫を全面的に改装したもの。築後50年を経た内部空間が持ち続けてきた大きなボリュームと、時代を経たことによる不思議な懐かしい感覚を大切にし、建物が呼吸してきた空気を表現することがデザインのコンセプトとされた。
そこで、既存の梁、柱、基礎の大部分はそのまま残され、そこに高い天井から吊り下げられ、風でゆらゆらと揺れる布張りの大きなペンダント照明、壁面に取り付けられたフォトパネルなど、今を感じさせるデザインが少しミックスされ、これまでと変わらない雰囲気を内部空間に再現している。

Charbon

America Mura is a gathering place for fashionable young people in Osaka. To its west, in Kita-Horie, shops with a new sensibility have begun to spring up amid the old-style commercial district. To create the cafe-restaurant Charbon, a wooden, two-floor warehouse in a corner of Kita-Horie was completely remodeled.
The idea behind Charbon's design was preserving the 50-year-old building's large volume and its curious, nostalgic atmosphere. Most of the existing foundation, beams and pillars were left in place. Large, cloth-covered pendant lights that sway in the breeze were hung from the high ceiling. Photo panels were affixed to the walls. This interior design revives the original atmosphere of the old building, while mixing in a few elements of the present.

1. 道路から開口部ガラス面を通して見た1階客席夜景
2. 1階右奥カフェテラス客席からカフェレストラン方向を見る
3. 2階から吹き抜けを通して見た1階カフェレストラン
4. 2階のバーカウンター席
5. 1階カフェレストラン客席から見たドリンクカウンター

1. A night view of the facade
2. A view of the cafe restaurant seating on the first floor
3. A down view of the cafe restaurant seating on the first floor
4. A view of the bar counter on the second floor
5. A view of the drink fountain on the first floor

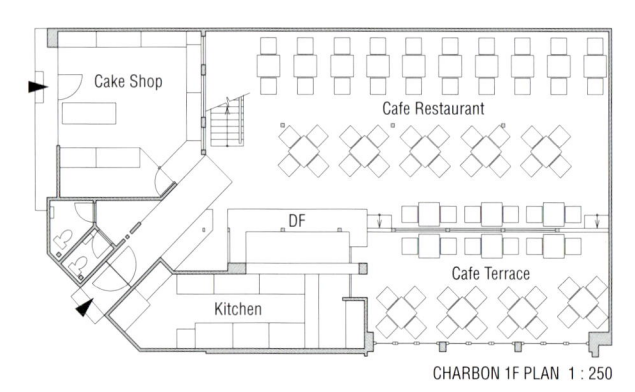

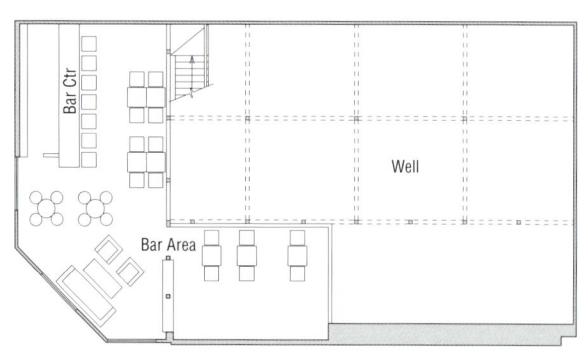

CHARBON 1F PLAN 1:250

2F PLAN

新業態としてのカフェ・キュイジーヌ

Cafe-Cuisine NEUT.

ニュートラル

大阪・曾根崎新地

Sonezaki-shinchi
Designer: Akira Gondo
Photographer: Seiryo Yamada

設 計：ギルド
施 工：TCネットワークス

1

2

3

華やかさとカジュアルさをミックス

JR大阪駅を中心とした繁華街・キタの一角に曾根崎新地はある。社用族を対象とした高級飲み屋街であるこの地域にも時代の波は押し寄せ、近隣の西梅田再開発などで従来とは違う客層が流入し始めたため、ボツボツと新しいタイプの店が見られるようになった。「ニュートラル」もそのような店の一つで、30歳前後の女性客をターゲットに、夜でも女性ひとりで気軽に利用できる新しい業態"夜カフェ"を目指している。

店づくりに関しては、この場所の遺伝子を少し受け継いだかたちで、華やかさと、カジュアルではあるが気取りを併せ持つデザインが採り入れられた。道路に面した1階内部のカフェとカウンターバーはスパンコールの付いたカーテンを垂らしてキラキラ感を演出し、階段を降りた地下1階のダイニングは、古レンガと塗装仕上げのコンクリート構造体によりニューヨーク的な活気を表現している。また、パーティー用にも使える地下1階奥のソファ席はバックライトの照明効果により、妖しくサロン的な雰囲気とされた。

Neutral

The neighborhood known as Sonezaki-shinchi is located in a corner of the commercial district Kita, which is centered around Japan Rail's Osaka Station. This neighborhood of high-grade bars that target expense-account spenders has run up against current conditions, and a new type of customer has come into the area – a trend encouraged by the redevelopment of neighboring Nishi-Umeda. To serve these new customers, new types of restaurants have gradually begun to appear.

Neutral is one such establishment. Targetting women around the age of 30, it was designed as a "night cafe," a new type of business for people who are happy to go out alone.

The shop's design inherits the heritage of the area, but also affects gaiety and casualness. The cafe and counter bar located on the first floor, facing the street, incorporate curtains that sparkle with dangling spangles. Downstairs, the dining area on the first underground floor is composed of old bricks and coated concrete that express a New York-style vigor. The back section of the first underground floor, which is sometimes used for parties, is distinguished by sofa seating and backlighting effects that create a dubious, salonlike ambiance.

1. テラス席から見た外観夜景
2. ミラー貼りのアプローチゲートから見た入り口まわり
3. 1階右側ソファ席からドリンクカウンター方向を見る
4. 1階と地下1階を結ぶ階段まわり
5. ロフト風の地下1階客席
6. アクリルミラーをランダムに貼り付けた地下1階のソファ席まわり壁面

1. A night view of the facade from the terrace seating
2. A view of the entrance from the mirror gate
3. A view of the staircase and drink fountain on the first floor
4. A view of the staircase
5. A view of the seating on the first basement floor
6. A view of the sofa seating on the first basement floor

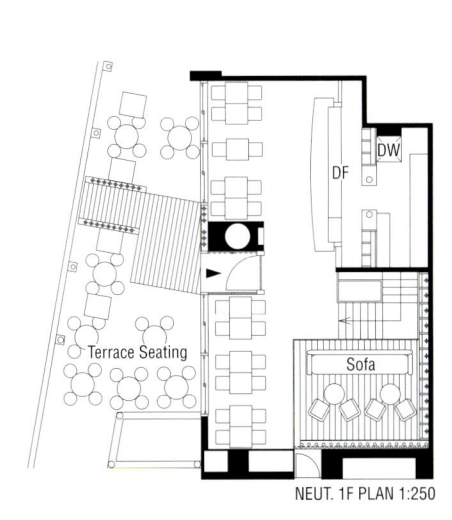

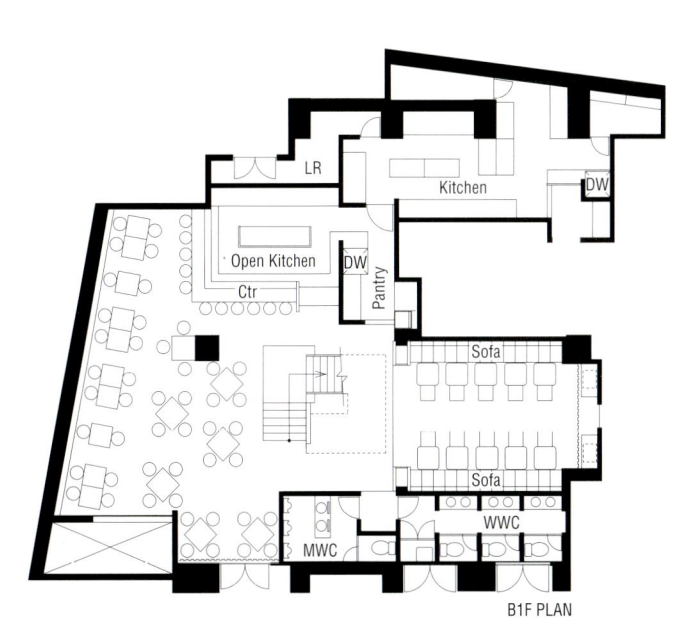

NEUT. 1F PLAN 1:250

B1F PLAN

地域の日常生活に密着したキッチン&カフェ　　Kitchen & Cafe QUEEN'S COURT

クィーンズコート

大阪・東大阪

Higashi-osaka, Osaka
Designer: Yasutoshi Mifune
Photographer: Seiryo Yamada

設 計： 美船デザインスタジオ
施 工： 大新建設工業

4

1. オープンカフェから見た開放的な入り口まわり
2. カウンター席奥から入り口側ベンチ席方向を見る
3. 入り口側ベンチ席の壁面と照明器具
4. 入り口から見た店内全景

1. A view of the entrance from the open cafe
2. A view from the counter to the bench seating
3. A view of the wall and lighting fixtures on the bench seating
4. A whole view of the interior from the entrance

細長い空間を居心地良くするデザイン

大阪の郊外、近鉄奈良線・東花園駅から徒歩1分の場所に「クィーンズコート」はある。地域に密着し、朝食やランチを提供するだけでなく、子供を学校などに送り出した主婦たちの溜まり場としても地元の人々に利用されてきた。店としては好立地だが、前面の道路から約9mセットバックしたビルの1階に位置し、間口が狭く奥行きが細長いという不利な条件を、いかにカバーするかが店づくりの課題であった。

そこで、狭い間口のファサードは、全面を開け放つことのできる透明ガラスの扉とすることで前面のオープンカフェとの一体感を出し、道路から店内が見通せる構成とされた。また、内部空間には浮遊感のあるステンレス製照明器具を吊り下げて天井の高さを強調し、来店客が空間にダイナミックさと開放感を感じられるようにデザインされた。

Queen's Court

Queen's Court is located in an Osaka suburb, a minute's walk from Higashi-hanazono Station on the Kintetsu Nara Line. Firmly established in the area, this cafe serves breakfast and lunch, and is a gathering spot for area homemakers who stop in after dropping their children off at school. The suburb is a good business location, but Queen's Court's is on the first floor of a building set back from the road about 9 meters. It has little frontage and is long and narrow.

To compensate, a small facade was built out of transparent glass doors that can be thrown open to expose the front cafe. This configuration makes the interior visible from the road.

Inside, stainless steel lighting fixtures suspended from the ceiling to emphasize its height seem to float in the air, and the overall design gives customers a feeling of dynamism and openness.

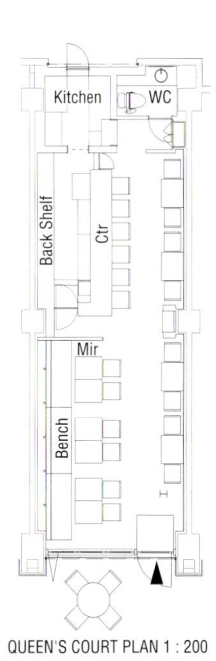

QUEEN'S COURT PLAN 1 : 200

個性的なロードサイド型コーヒー&グリルバー

Coffee & Grill BREAK

ブレーク
愛知・碧南市

Hekinan, Aichi
Designer: Shoichi Kanayama
Photographer: Seiryo Yamada

設計：ボーイ・カンパニー
施工：創シンコー
　　　ハヤシ建設巧芸

空間を和らげる円柱形の照明

名古屋の郊外，知多半島の東側に面する碧南市にできた「ブレーク」は，市役所や警察署に隣接し，周囲はロードサイドスタイルの大型飲食店が建ち並ぶ環境であった。魅力あるレストランやバーなどが皆無であったことから，個性あるリラックス空間をコンセプトに店づくりが進められた。建物は2階建てで，1階はテナントが入り，2階がこの店である。

建物の外観デザインに関しては，あまりデコラティブにならないよう，ストレートでシンプルなディテールでまとめられた。また，内部デザインは，あえて無機質なステンレスやクロームメッキ仕上げの金物を多用し，シャープでクールな空間を演出。それらに対比するものとして木製格子組みの飾り棚を中央に設置し，円柱形の照明柱と組み合わせることで柔らかな雰囲気を付加している。

Break

Break is located in the Nagoya suburb of Hekinan City, which faces the east side of the Chita Peninsula. This coffee shop and grill is adjacent to the city hall and police department near several large, roadside-style eating and drinking establishments. Because the area had no restaurants and bars with any charm, a design concept of an individualistic space where customers could relax was recommended.

Break is on the second-floor of a two-story building, with another tenant on the first floor. The exterior of the building is characterized by direct, simple details and a lack of ornamentation. Break's bold interior makes abundant use of inorganic stainless steel and chrome-finished hardware, to produce a sharp, cool space. Wooden, lattice display shelves placed in the center and cylindrical light pillars provide a contrast and add a soft ambiance.

1. 入り口からレジカウンターを通して店内を見る
2. 道路から見たビル外観。ブレークは2階に位置する
3. グリルバー客席奥のステンレス製壁面間接照明
4. グリルバー客席から見た奥の飾り棚と円柱形照明柱
5. 円柱形照明柱からグリルバー客席を見る

1. A view from the entrance to the inner part
2. An evening view of the building facade
3. A view of the indirect lighting wall in the grill bar
4. A view of the lighting shelves from the grill bar
5. A view of the grill bar from the lighting shelves

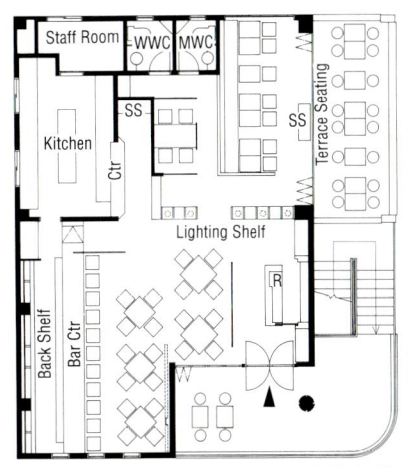

BREAK PLAN 1 : 250

ホテル1階角地のダイニングカフェ

Dining & Cafe VIS-A-VIS

ヴィ サ ヴィ
大阪・大融寺

Taiyuji-cho, Osaka
Designer: Shigemasa Noi
Photographer: Seiryo Yamada

設 計： 野井成正デザイン事務所
施 工： 吉野創美

1. 入り口右側客席から見たバーカウンターまわり
2. キッチンカウンター左端から奥方向を見る
3. 左隅コーナーからキッチンカウンター方向を見る
4. 店内奥から見たキッチンカウンター全景

1. A view of the bar counter from the right corner
2. A view of the kitchen counter to the inmost part
3. A view from the left corner to the kitchen counter
4. A whole view of the kitchen counter

オープンキッチンを取り囲む空間構成

大阪の繁華街・キタの中心から少し離れた場所にあるホテル1階に「ヴィ サ ヴィ」は計画された。前が太融寺というお寺で、その塀や境内の木々が見えるという繁華街には珍しい静けさが感じられる一角である。その立地条件を生かし、道路に面した2面を総ガラス張りとし、街の風景を取り込んだ開放的で清潔な店づくりが志向された。

店内のデザインは「火と熱」の演出を主眼とし、中央の大きなオープンキッチンによって来客は料理が作られていく手順や動きを間近に見ながら、匂いや熱気、音を感じ、臨場感を楽しむことができる。

また、夜になると天井からワイヤーでランダムに吊り下げられた薄いアルミパンチングの反射板に照明が当たって輝き、光のきらめきやゆらめき、光と影のグラデーションが来客の会話を弾ませる。

Vis á Vis

Vis á Vis is located on the first floor of a hotel a short distance from the center of the Kita commercial district in Osaka. A temple called Taiyuji stands in front of the hotel, and the view of the temple wall and the trees behind it give the spot a tranquility that is rare in commercial areas. To take advantage of this location, the designer made the two walls facing the street all glass to create an open, clean design that incorporates the surrounding scenery.

The main ideas of the interior design are "fire and heat." An open kitchen in the center allows customers a close view of the process and movements involved in preparing their food and lets them experience the associated smells, heat and sounds. At night, lights are shone on reflective, punched aluminum boards hung randomly from the ceiling with wire, causing them to gleam and flicker. The resulting gradations of light and shadow seem to urge on customers' conversations.

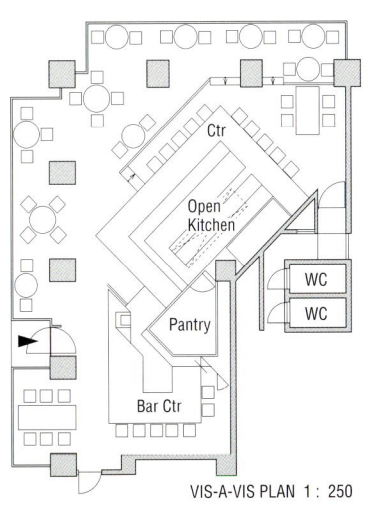

VIS-A-VIS PLAN 1 : 250

CAFE-RESTAURANTS

デリ併設のティー・ダイニング

パリヤ 北青山
東京・北青山

Tea, Dining & Bar **PARIYA Kita-aoyama**

Kita-aoyama, Tokyo
Designer: Mayumi Kanmi
Photographer: Hiro Photo

設 計： 官見真弓デザイン事務所
施 工： ジェイズ プランニング

ミステリアスでグラマラスなデザイン

東京・青山の裏通りにできた「パリヤ」は，従来はジェラートとランチタイムにのみ弁当を販売する店として地域の人に親しまれてきた。しかし，入居していたビルが取り壊されることになり，近くに移転して，「気取らず入れる大人の空間」を店づくりのコンセプトにしたデリ併設のレストランとなった。
メゾネットタイプの住居用マンション1，2階にある2戸分を改装した店舗は，人通りの少ない道路に面しているため，ファサード自体がこの通りのランドマークになり，通行人の記憶に残るデザインが志向された。店内は，ブティックを経営し，ファッションデザイナーでもあるオーナーのテイストを生かし，ミステリアスでグラマラスな美を表現することが試みられた。

Pariya

Pariya, built on a back street in Aoyama, Tokyo, was beloved by locals for its gelato and for its boxed lunches served only at lunchtime. When Pariya's building was scheduled for demolition, it was rebuilt in a nearby location as a restaurant and delicatessen. The design theme was "a casual space for adults."
Pariya occupies two apartments' worth of remodeled space on the first and second floor of a maisonette-type residential apartment house. Because it faces a street with little pedestrian traffic, its facade was designed to be memorable and has become a landmark on the street. The interior design makes good use of the tastes of the owner - a fashion designer who manages a boutique – and aims to express a mysterious, glamorous beauty.

1. 道路から見たファサード夜景
2. 1階左側客席を入り口側から見る
3. 1階の銅板貼りデリコーナー壁面
4. 1階入り口左側客席から右側客席方向を見る

1. A night view of the facade
2. A view of the left side seating on the first floor
3. A view of the deli counter on the first floor
4. A view of the entrance and display table on the first floor

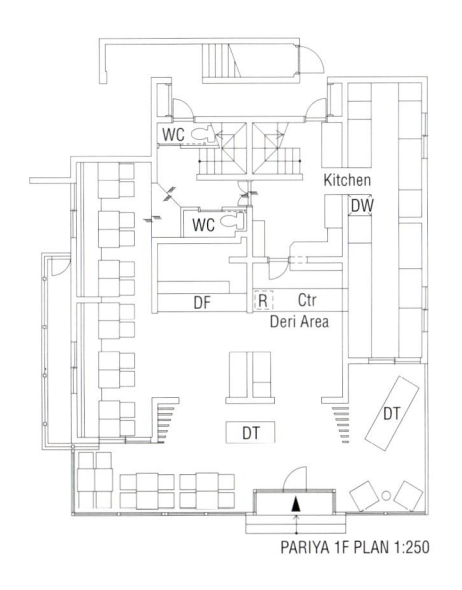

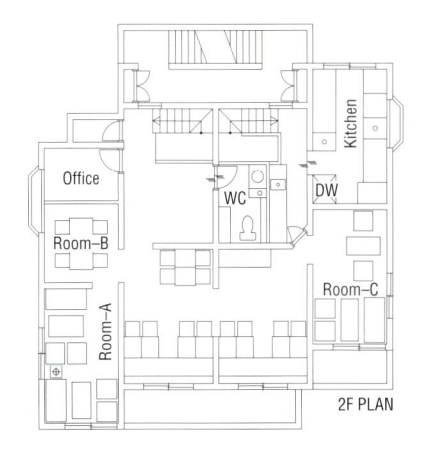

PARIYA 1F PLAN 1:250

2F PLAN

食空間とモータースポーツを融合させる

Cafe & Restaurant **GRIGRIA BACS CAFE**

グリグリア バックス カフェ

東京・六本木

Roppongi, Tokyo
Designer: Masahiro Shiomi
Photographer: Satoshi Asakawa

設計：ビス・アティック
施工：オカベ

サーキットのピット裏空間を再現

東京・六本木の交差点近くにあるビルの地下にできた「グリグリア バックス カフェ」は、カー用品専門店を全国に展開する企業の新規事業第1号店である。"車"と"食"という不釣り合いなこの組み合わせを、どのように融合させるかが今回の店づくりの大きなポイントであった。

店内のデザインは、クライアント側からのレースカーサーキットの雰囲気を出してほしいという要望から、以前は車庫として使用されていたアプローチ部分にサーキットのピットのイメージを再現し、実際にレースで走行していたレースカーがディスプレイされた。また、中央のカフェ・エリア、および、奥のレストラン・エリアには、デザインマテリアルとしてステンレスやアルミなどのメタリックな素材、エンジン、アルミホイール、マフラー、フロントグリルなどの車の部品が使われている。

Grigria Bacs Cafe

Grigria Bacs Cafe, located in the basement of a building near an intersection in Roppongi, Tokyo, is the first foray into new businesses for a company that builds automotive accessory shops throughout Japan. An important point in the design of Grigria Bacs Cafe was how to fuse the two discordant concepts of cars and food.

The client asked the interior designer to create the atmosphere of a race car circuit, so a racecourse pit was re-created in the restaurant's approach section, which used to be a garage. A race car actually driven in races is displayed there.

For the central cafe and rear restaurant, metallic materials such as stainless steel and aluminum were chosen. Decorations include engines, aluminum wheels, mufflers, grilles and other car parts.

1. レーシングカーを飾ってある入り口アプローチまわり夜景
2. 入り口から奥方向へカフェ全景を見る
3. レストラン客席壁面を飾るカーホイールキャップ
4. 店内奥のレストラン個室への通路
5. 奥にあるレストランのカウンターキッチン側から見た客席

1. A night view of the entrance with race car
2. A whole view of the cafe from the entrance
3. A view of the restaurant wall with car wheel cap
4. A view of the passage to the restaurant room
5. A view of the seating from the counter kitchen side

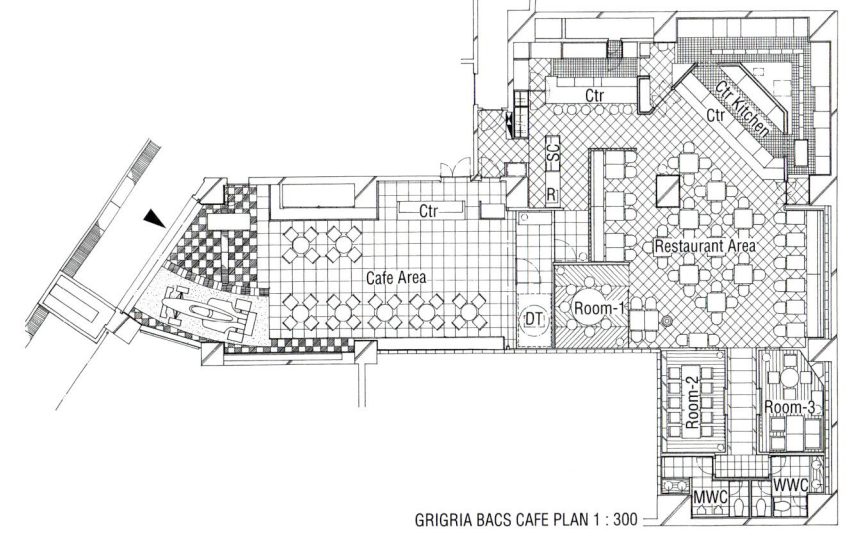

GRIGRIA BACS CAFE PLAN 1 : 300

お台場の巨大ビル内にあるカフェ&レストラン

Cafe BALCONY

バルコニー
東京・有明

Ariake, Tokyo
Designer: Masahito Miyazaki
Photographer: Satoshi Asakawa

設計：フォルテ建築設計事務所
施工：中央設備エンジニアリング

1

日常的なインテリジェンスを空間に演出

通称"お台場"と呼ばれている東京臨海副都心地区にあるホテル日航東京が、外部進出第1号として同じお台場にある巨大商業ビルに出店したのが「バルコニー」である。店づくりに関しては、ホテルのコンセプトである"自然、やすらぎ、インテリジェンス"を訪れる人にアピールできることが、クライアント側からの要望であった。
そこで、店内のデザインは、ホテルと同様に木材、石材を中心とした自然素材で全体が構成された。しかし、ディテールのデザイン、利用の仕方に関しては、よりモダンな手法を採り入れ、ホテルとは一味違うカジュアルで"日常的なインテリジェンス"が感じられる空間に仕上げられた。

Balcony

Hotel Nikko Tokyo, located in a section of Rinkai-Fukutoshin nicknamed "Odaiba," opened Balcony in an enormous Odaiba commercial building as its first outside venture. The owner wanted the cafe's design to appeal to people drawn to the hotel's design theme of "nature, tranquility and intelligence."
The interior was built using natural materials including wood and stone, just like the hotel. However, the designer included original details, used the materials in a different way and adopted more modern methods, creating a casual space with an "everyday intelligence" slightly removed from the ambiance of the hotel.

1. 入り口左側の飾り棚わきから見たソファ席全景
2. 奥のテラス席からソファ席方向を見る
3. ビルのルーフデッキに面したテラス席
4. ビルの通路から見た入り口まわり

1. A view of the sofa seating from the entrance
2. A view of the sofa seating from the terrace seating
3. A view of the terrace seating facing the building roof deck
4. A view of the entrance from the building passage

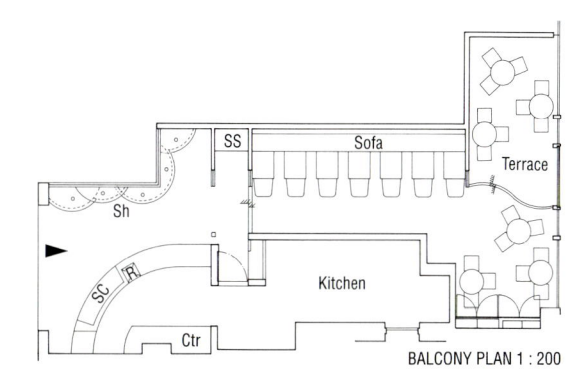

BALCONY PLAN 1 : 200

和食店を震災後にカフェ&レストランとして再建

ちから
神戸・上沢通り

Cafe & Restaurant **CHIKARA**

Kamisawa-doori, Kobe
Designer: Daisaku Takahashi
Photographer: Seiryo Yamada

設計：設計工房タカハシ
施工：分離発注方式

女性好みの柔らかな光と雰囲気

神戸・湊川は中心繁華街ではないが，昔からの街並みが残り，新しいマンションなども混在する地域である。地下鉄・湊川駅近くにできた「ちから」は，以前にオーナーの生家が和食の大衆食堂「力餅」を営んでいた場所に計画された。生家は阪神大震災による災害で再開発ビルとして建て直され，その1階に跡を継いだ息子が新しい店をオープンさせたわけである。

店づくりは，女性を対象としたカフェ＆レストランということもあり，自己主張の強いマテリアルを避け，ニュートラルな空間づくりが志向された。店内を特徴づけているのは，奥のソファ席壁面に設けられている円形にくり抜かれた間接照明と，入り口側のカウンター席上部のスクエアな照明器具で，その対比が空間に女性好みの柔らかな光と雰囲気を生み出している。

Chikara

Minatogawa, Kobe, is not a central commercial district, but an area with old streets of houses and shops, and new apartment buildings mixed in. Chikara is located near the Minatogawa subway station in a spot where the owner's parents formerly operated the popular dining hall Chikaramochi. The building that housed his parents' establishment was rebuilt after the Great Hanshin Earthquake, and the owner opened Chikara on the new building's first floor to follow in his parents' footsteps.

Partly because this cafe and restaurant targets women, ostentatious materials were avoided in the interior design, and the creation of a neutral space was emphasized.

The interior is distinguished by indirect lighting placed in circular holes in the walls of the rear table-seating area, and by square lighting equipment above the counter seating. These contrasting fixtures combine to create the type of soft light and ambiance favored by women.

---

1. 奥のアール壁に面した客席
2. 入り口まわり夜景
3. 奥右側ソファ席から見たアール壁側客席
4. アール壁側客席からカウンター席方向を見る
5. キッチン側から見たソファ席と柔らかな光を放つ壁面間接照明

1. A view of the seating with curved wall
2. A night view of the entrance
3. A view of the seating with curved wall from the sofa seating
4. A view of the counter seating from the curved wall side
5. A view of the sofa seating and indirect lighting wall

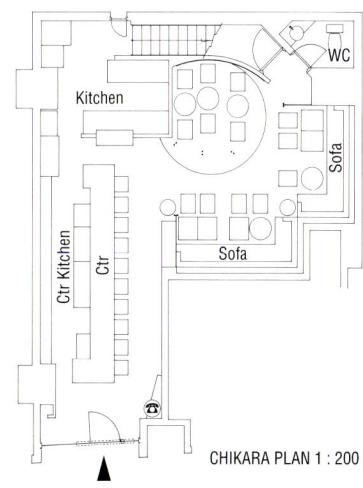

CHIKARA PLAN 1 : 200

カフェ・レストラン・バーの多毛作店

イズントイット お初天神店

大阪・曾根崎

Cafe, Restaurant & Bar ISN'T IT? Ohatsu-tenjin

Sonezaki, Osaka
Producer: Koichi Yoshikawa
Photographer: Yoshihisa Araki

設 計：ノモス
施 工：ヤマケイ

時間により業態を変化させる工夫

大阪・キタの繁華街にできた「イズントイット」は、新しいカフェの業態を開発し、チェーン展開を図っているプロデュース会社が計画した。朝から夕方まではカフェとレストラン、夜はレストランバー、深夜はDJクラブという具合に業態を変化させながら、店舗を一日中フルに活用するのが、店のコンセプトである。

この店の場合は、さらにテーブルが動き、フロアが移動するという新しい試みがなされた。3台のテーブルは状況に応じてくっついたり、離れたりするだけでなく、テーブルトップが跳ね上がって壁に掛かった絵のような状態になる。また、道路側のカフェ客席は床全体がスライドしてフロントサイドのステージに迫り出し、オープンカフェとなる。

Isn't It? Ohatsu-tenjin

Isn't It, located in the commercial district of Kita, Osaka, was created by a production company that is developing a chain of cafes based on a new business model. The idea behind these establishments is to operate throughout the day by serving as a cafe and restaurant from morning to evening, as a restaurant and bar at night and as a DJ club late at night.

In the case of Isn't It, moveable tables and floors were added as a new experiment. The three tables not only can be combined or separated as needed, their tabletops can be hung like paintings on the wall. Moreover, the entire floor of the cafe seating area near the road can be slid over to form a stage and create an open cafe.

1. 道路側に迫り出した状態のテラス席夜景
2. レジ側から見たテラス席
3. 店内右奥の客席。壁面側のテーブルは壁に折り畳める
4. 奥のDJブースとドリンクカウンター

1. A night view of the moving terrace floor
2. A view of the terrace seating from the cashier side
3. A view of the inmost seating with tables folding on the wall
4. A view of the DJ booth and drink counter

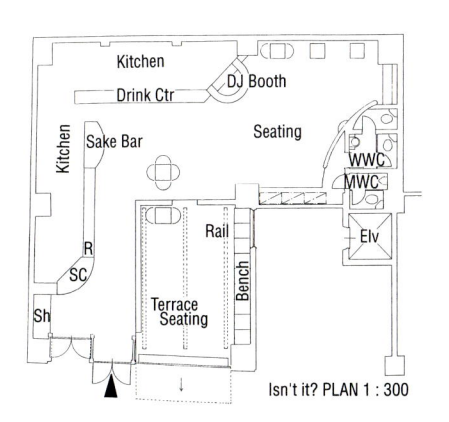

Isn't it? PLAN 1 : 300

三つの業態が一つの空間で同時進行するカフェ | Cafe LAISSER

レゼ
大阪・和泉市

Izumi, Osaka
Designer: Akira Gondo
Photographer: Seiryo Yamada

設 計： ギルド　石井工務店
施 工： 石井工務店

ガラスナギットによる鮮やかな透過光

大阪南部のベッドタウン・和泉市は、近年、大学やマンションが建ち、ヤングファミリーや大学生といった流入人口の多い地域である。将来は幹線道路になるであろう広い通りに面してはいるが、周囲は未だ田圃の多い開発途中の地区に「レゼ」はオープンした。

のどかな土地柄を考え、来客がそのときの気分でカフェ、イタリア料理、バー、パーティーなどを自由に選択し、一つの店で三つの業態が時間帯の区別なく共存し、同時進行しながら楽しめるというのが店づくりのコンセプトであった。

ポップなオモチャ箱のようなファサードは近隣に異彩を放っており、また、内部空間ではカウンターバックに配された3色のガラスナギットが、メルヘンチックな光り壁を構成し、この地域に新しくやってきた若い人たちを迎える。

Laisser

Izumi is a bedroom community to the south of Osaka. A university and apartment buildings were built there in recent years, and the area has a mobile population that includes many young families and college students.

The cafe Laisser faces a road likely to become a main thoroughfare in a developing area that still has a lot of rice paddies.

In consideration of the quietness of the area and customers who freely choose among cafes, Italian restaurants, bars, parties and the like based on their whims, the owner chose a design that would allow Laisser to operate three types of business at the same time.

The facade, which is reminiscent of a toy box, displays conspicuous colors to the surrounding neighborhood. Inside, tricolor glass nuggets are arranged behind the counter to make up a lighted wall with a fairy tale quality. This display greets the young people who have recently moved to the area when they enter Laisser.

1. 道路からテラス席を通して見た外観
2. 1階カウンター席から見たソファ席
3. ガラスナギットを貼り付けたカウンターバック
4. 1階ソファ席から見たカウンター席
5. 入り口から見た1階客席全景
6. 2階パーティールーム

1. A view of the entrance from the street
2. A view of the sofa seating from the counter on the first floor
3. A view of the counter back wall with glass nuggets
4. A view of the counter from the sofa seating on the first floor
5. A whole view of the interior from the entrance on the first floor
6. A view of the party room on the second floor

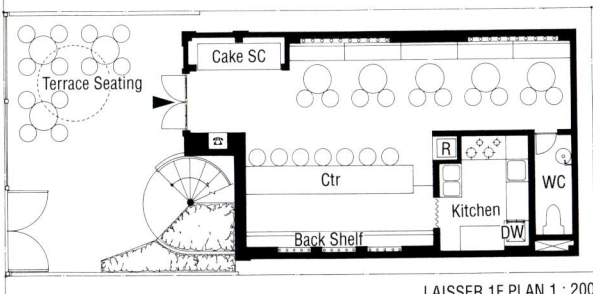

LAISSER 1F PLAN 1 : 200

2F PLAN

コミュニティーを目指す住宅併用ダイニングカフェ

屯風
京都・高野泉町

Dining & Cafe TON-FU

Takano-izumicho, Kyoto
Designer: Yoshiteru Uesato
Photographer: Seiryo Yamada

設 計：聖拙社
施 工：施主直営

1. 入り口から見た大テーブル席
2. 道路から見た外観
3. 入り口右側にある2階住居への階段を大テーブル席から見る
4. 大テーブル席から奥のカウンター席方向を見る
5. 店内中央から見た奥のカウンター席
6. 最奥部にある個室内部

1. A view of the big table from the entrance
2. A view of the facade from the street
3. A view from the big table to the staircase
4. A view from the big table side to the counter seating
5. A view of the counter from the center
6. An interior view of the inmost room

仲間たちとの手作り作業で完成した空間

京都の外れ、一乗寺界隈には以前「京一会館」という映画館があり、地区の娯楽と文化の一端を担っていた。「屯風」は無くなって久しい映画館の代わりに、地区のコミュニティー的な存在となることを目指して出発した。オーナーのかつて17年間勤めた店が、地域に根ざし、仲間が集まってくるような店であったことから発想されたものである。店づくりに際しては「風が通るように」、「光が入るように」、「坪庭を設ける」という具体的な要望が出された。それらを実現しながら、さらにカフェ＆バーとしての機能、ダイニングとしての機能、仲間たちの溜まり場としての位置付けが検討された。そして、オーナーおよび仲間たち自らの手作り作業により、7カ月の長い施工期間を経て「屯風」は完成した。

Ton-Fu

The neighborhood of Ichijoji temple on the outskirts of Kyoto used to be home to a movie theater called Kyoichi-kaikan, which contributed entertainment and culture to the area. Ton-Fu was designed as a community establishment to replace this movie theater, which disappeared long ago. The cafe-bar and restaurant was conceived by the owner, who worked at the restaurant-bar for 17 years and remembers it as a place with roots in the community and as a gathering spot for friends.

The owner had three specific elements he wanted to incorporate in Ton-Fu's design: breeze, sunlight and a small garden. So he and his friends examined how to accomplish this while also achieving functionality as a cafe, bar, restaurant and gathering spot. They built Ton-Fu themselves over the course of seven months – a relatively long construction period.

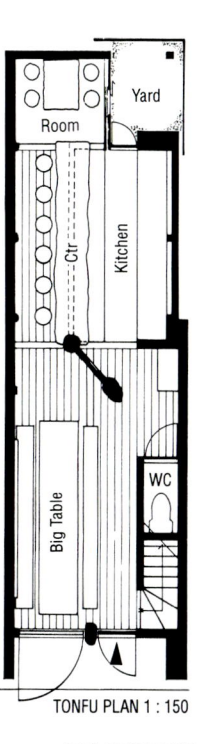

TONFU PLAN 1 : 150

老舗の伝統をモダンに再現したリニューアル

資生堂パーラー 横浜そごう店

横浜・高島

Restaurant Cafe **SHISEIDO PARLOUR Yokohama-sogo**

Takashima, Yokohama
Designer: Stomu Ushidate
Photographer: Nacása & Partners

設 計：牛建 務＋
　　　 インタースペースタイム
施 工：ヴイアート

1

和と洋のエッセンスを籐で表現

資生堂パーラーの本店は東京・銀座にあり、オープンしてから100年近い歴史を誇る日本でも有数の老舗レストランである。横浜そごう店はデパートの2階にあり、開店以来10年目にリニューアルされた。間口が広く、奥行きのない空間形状に変化を持たせること、アットホームな感じの木質のデザインにすることが改装に際して要望された。

もともと、本店が和と洋の持つエッセンスをうまく調和させたデザインであったことから、この店の場合は籐という素材が使用されることとなった。ランダムな方向に織り上げられた籐のスクリーンは背後が透けて見える構造であり、入り口部分から客席方向への視線と、外部のパブリックなテラスからの視線を半ば遮りながら、奥の客席の雰囲気が透き間越しに感じられるようになっている。

Shiseido Parlour Yokohama-sogo

The Ginza, Tokyo main location of Shiseido Parlour is one of the few restaurants in Japan that boasts a near 100-year history.

The Yokohama Sogo outlet, located on the second floor of the department store Sogo, was remodeled 10 years after it opened. The objectives of the remodeling were to change the shape of the interior, which was wide but had little depth, and to implement a homey design that uses a lot of wood.

The original interior design of the Ginza main location stressed a harmony of the East and the West. So rattan was chosen as a building material for the Yokohama outlet. Rattan branches twine upward in random directions, interweaving to form screens that partially block the view of the customer seating area from the entrance and from the public terrace outside. But the seating area and its atmosphere can still be glimpsed through the crevices.

1. 入り口から店内右側のソファ席を見る。
   壁面スクリーンとパーティションは
   籐をランダムに編んだもの
2. デパートの屋外ルーフデッキから
   スクリーン越しに見た店内
3. ルーフデッキ側から見た店内右側客席

1. A view of the sofa seating from the entrance
2. A view from the department store roof deck to the waiting area
3. A view of the right side seating from the window side

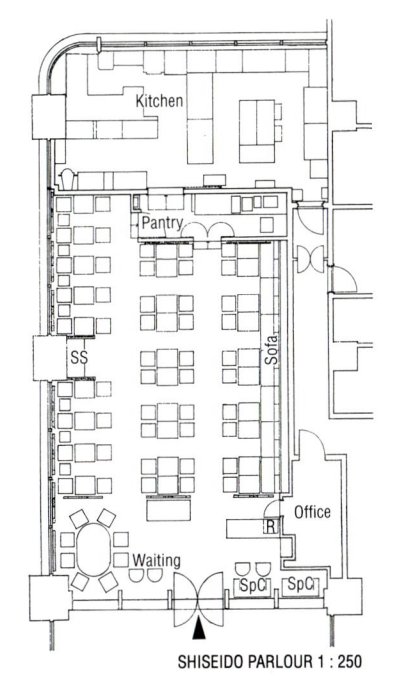

SHISEIDO PARLOUR 1 : 250

ビル屋上のガーデンダイニング＆カフェ

束矢亭
東京・玉川

Garden Dining & Cafe **TABAYATEI**

Tamagawa, Tokyo
Designer: Shin Oohori
Photographer: Nacása & Partners

設計：インテンショナリーズ
施工：ファブユニバーサル

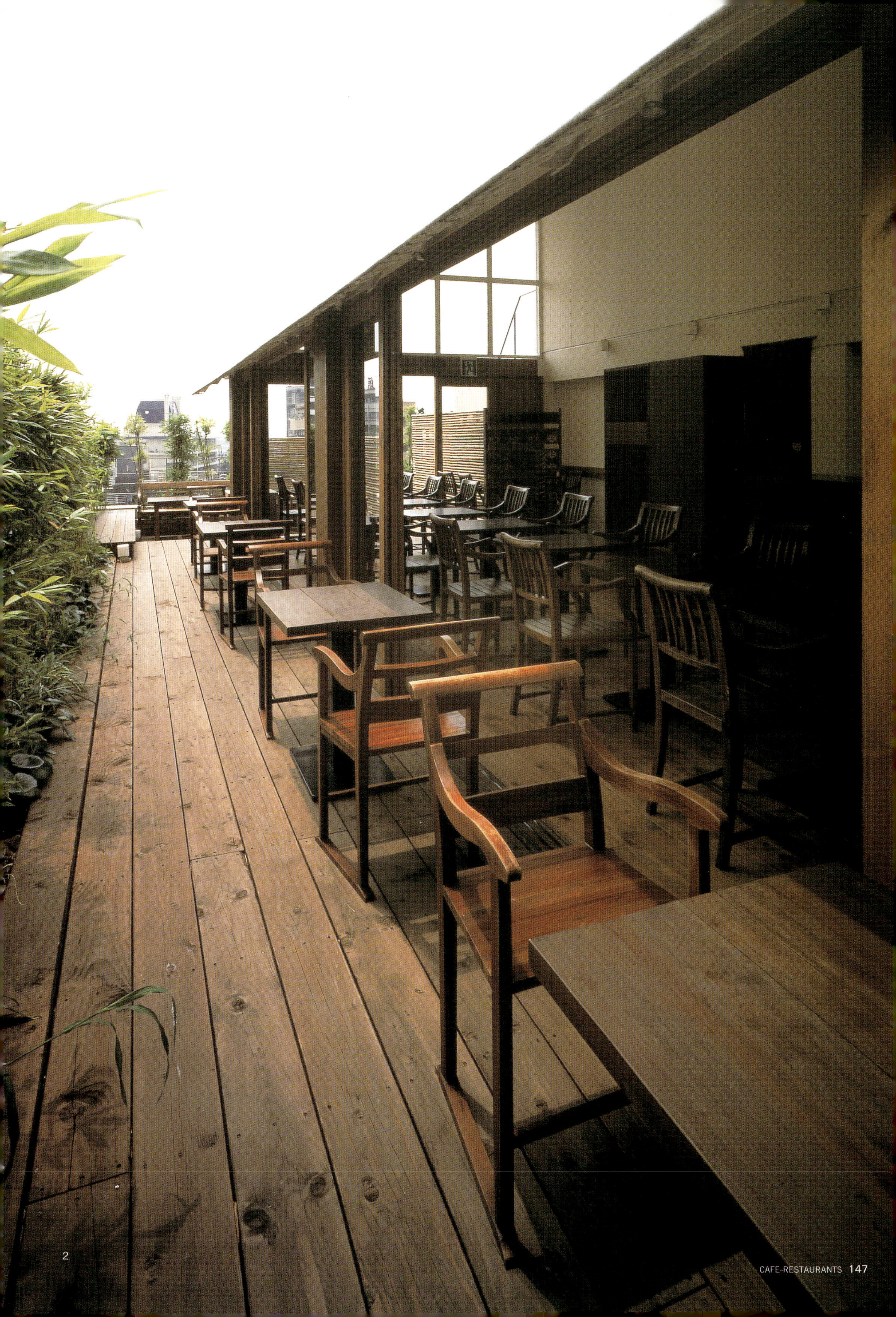

2

和をベースにしたアジアンテイスト

東京の高級住宅地・玉川にある商業ビル5階の屋上を利用した屋外感覚のレストランである。玉川の中心・玉川高島屋SCに隣接しているが周囲の景色が良くないため，竹林が目隠しとしてビルのフェンスに沿って植えられ，竹に囲まれた独自の空気が感じられるニュートラルな雰囲気の"場"が構成された。和をベースとしたアジア的なテイストがショップコンセプトであり，料理もそれに沿ったメニューが用意されている。
既存の鉄骨を利用して作られた屋根は風雨を防ぐための簡単な構造とされ，天気の良い日は空を眺めることのできる可動式のテントが取り付けられた。また，外部テラスに面した壁全体を開放できるよう，木製サッシのスライディングドアが採用された。外部テラスはオープンエアで食事のできる客席とされ，内部客席同様に明るい光と心地よい風を楽しみながら快適なひとときを来店客は過ごすことができる。

Tabayatei

Tabayatei is a partially outdoor restaurant on the fifth-floor roof of a commercial building in the high-class residential neighborhood of Tamagawa, Tokyo. The building is adjacent to the central shopping center Tamagawa Takashimaya. But because the surrounding scenery is unappealing, bamboo thickets were planted along the fence to block it from sight. The result was a bamboo-enclosed spot with an original but neutral atmosphere. The design concept of Tabayatei is an Asian sensibility rooted in Japan. The menu follows the same theme. A moveable tent was built using the existing roof frame to protect diners from the wind and rain but allow them to gaze at the sky when the weather is fair. Wood-framed sliding doors can be opened to expose the outdoor terrace. Customers can experience open-air dining at the tables on the outdoor terrace, and can enjoy sunlight and a comfortable breeze while dining indoors as well.

1. ルーフデッキ奥のテラス席から見た外観夜景
2. 竹林に囲まれたルーフデッキ上のテラス席。ドアを開け放してオープンにした状態
3. 店内から屋外のテラス席方向を見る
4. ビルの屋上に建てられた外観夜景
5. 待合から見たテラスのベンチ席

1. A view from the inmost terrace seating to the interior
2. A view of the open-air terrace seating surrounded with bamboo
3. A view from the interior to the open-air terrace seating
4. A view of the facade on the building roof
5. A view of the terrace bench seating from the waiting area

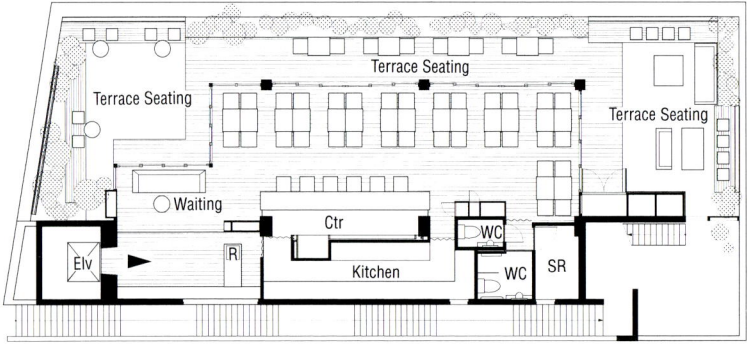

TABAYATEI PLAN 1 : 250

CHAPTER 4
ショップデータ

データ内容は月刊商店建築掲載時のものです

第1章 複合カフェ

● インディヴィ カフェ (6P)
所在地：東京都新宿区西新宿1-1-3 小田急百貨店新宿本館2階
工事種別：内装のみ 全面改装
床面積114.4m²
工期：1997年10月6日〜10月29日
*営業内容
開店：1997年11月1日
営業時間：午前10時〜午後7時30分
定休日：不定休(火曜日)
電話：(03)3344-6372
経営者：小田急デパートサービス(株)
従業員数：サービス15人 厨房2人 合計17人
客席数：48席 客単価：836円
客回転数：3.8回
主なメニューと単価：コーヒー・紅茶600〜 ケーキセット950〜 ランチセット1150〜
*主な仕上げ材料
床：ライムストーン貼り水磨き ファサード部分／ココヤシカーペット
壁：PBt12セメント系薄塗り材塗布 一部ライムストーン貼り水磨き アルミパネル貼りサンドブラスト仕上げ
天井：PBおよびボンデ鋼板セメント系薄塗り材塗布
家具・什器：カウンター／人造大理石 テーブル／ブラジリアンローズウッド材突き板
*商店建築'98-04号掲載

● カバ代官山店 (8P)
所在地：東京都渋谷区恵比寿1-35-17 DKビル代官山地下1階(現存せず)
工事種別：内装 全面改装
床面積：97.5m²
工期：1999年7月1日〜8月10日
*営業内容
開店：1999年8月21日
営業時間：午前10時〜午後9時
定休日：なし 電話：(03)3462-9176
経営者：(株)ル・ショップ
従業員：サービス10人 厨房2人 合計12人(うちアルバイト10人)
客席数：32席 客単価：750円
主なメニューと単価：ブレンドコーヒー400 アイスコーヒー450 スムージー600 生ハムのブレッドサラダ800 カバカレー900
*主な仕上げ材料
床：モルタル金ゴテ仕上げ
壁・天井：セメント系薄塗り材金ゴテ仕上げ 一部リブ付きアクリル＋乳半アクリル(FL内照式)
家具・什器：ベンチ／アルミアルマイト仕上げ角パイプ 一部ウレタン下地ホワイトレザー巻き付け カウンター／ステンレスヘアライン イス／オリジナル製作 冷蔵ショーケース／ステンレスメラミン焼き付けつや消し(白)＋クリアガラス＋ステンレス鏡面仕上げ
*商店建築'99-10月号掲載

● ミュゼ大阪 (11P)
所在地：大阪府大阪市西区南堀江1-21-7
工事種別：一戸建て 新築
用途地域地区：商業地域
建ぺい率：制限100％＞実効77％
容積率：制限600％＞実効210％
構造と規模：S造 地上3階建て
敷地面積：103m² 建築面積：80m²
床面積：1階80m²(うち厨房21m²) 2階56m² 3階80m²(うち厨房10m²) 合計216m²
工期：1998年6月13日〜9月30日
総工費：5000万円
*営業内容
開店：1998年10月3日
営業時間：カフェ／午前11時〜午後2時 ギャラリー／正午〜午後6時 サロン／午後5時〜午前2時
定休日：なし
電話：カフェ＆サロン(06)4391-3030 ギャラリー(06)4391-3031
経営者：(株)エル・ワールド
従業員：18人(うちパート11人)
客席数：77席 客単価：カフェ／昼1300円 夜3500円 サロン／5000円
客回転数：カフェ／4.5回 サロン／2.5回
主なメニューと単価：ミュゼ風ハンバーグ1000 ハッシュドビーフ1200 チーズプレート1200 カルボナーラ1000 ミュゼ・フルーツドリンク1000
*主なな仕上げ材料
屋根：軽鉄組みガルバリウム鋼板
外壁：白モルタル寒水入り金ゴテ押さえ 一部アピトン材フローリング染色木材保護着色剤塗布 開口部／スチール黒皮仕上げの上フッ素CL
外部床：コンクリートの上クリア防塵塗装
床：1階／コンクリートの上クリア防塵塗装 2階／杉板染色CL 3階／ジャラ材ワックス仕上げ
壁：PBt12EP塗装 一部アピトン材染色木材保護着色剤塗布 柱／白モルタル寒水入り金ゴテ押さえ
天井：PBt12EP塗装 一部木製リブ取り付け(3階)
什器：レセプションカウンター＆ビッグプランツボックス／銅板染色仕上げ 1階キッチンカウンター／大理石貼り 3階バーカウンター／チーク材染色ウレタンCL
*商店建築'99-01月号掲載

● チャロン[茶虫] (14P)
所在地：大阪府大阪市中央区博労町4-6-14 ラボ1階
工事種別：内装のみ 全面改装
床面積：83m²(うち厨房10m²)
工期：1988年7月1日〜8月27日
*営業内容
開店：1988年8月25日
営業時間：正午〜午後8時
定休日：第3水曜
電話：(06)6253-3310
経営者：(有)イン 従業員：3人
客席数：12席 客単価：600円
客回転：3回
主なメニューと単価：玄米茶400 赤ちゃん番茶400 牛乳煮込茶600 玄米ローストティー500 正山子種(中国茶)400
*主な仕上げ材料
床：杉板フローリング白染色
幅木：木質幅木(黒)
壁：PBt12AEP
家具・什器：別注
*商店建築'98-12月号掲載

● フランキーボーイカフェ (16P)
所在地：東京都渋谷区宇田川町16-17 イーストボーイユナイテッド本店3階(現存せず)
工事種別：内外装 全面改装
床面積：203m²(うち厨房33m²)
工期：1997年3月10日〜4月5日
*営業内容
開店：1997年4月5日
営業時間：午前11時〜午後8時
経営者：(株)イーストポイント
従桑員数：20人(うちパート18人)
客席数：80席 客単価：850円
客回転数：4回
主なメニューと単価：コーヒー400 ジューシービーフバーガー780 アメリカンホットドッグ550 アメリカンレモネード500 カシスビア600
*主な仕上げ材料
床：モザイクタイル貼り
壁：PBt12下地エマルション系薄塗り材 一部モザイクタイル貼り
天井：PBt9AEP
*商店建築'98-04月号掲載

● ティーパス (18P)
所在地：神奈川県茅ヶ崎市浜須賀2-7
工事種別：一戸建て 新築
用途地域地区：第2種中高層住居専用地域
建ぺい率：制限60％＞実効27.04％
容積率：制限200％＞実効21.80％
構造と規模：S造 平屋建て
敷地面積：362.67m²
建築面積：98.08m²
床面積：79.07m²(うち厨房18.49m²)
工期：1998年1月10日〜5月30日
総工費：3425万円
*営業内容
開店：1998年6月19日
営業時間：午前10時〜午後7時
定休日：火曜 電話：(0467)82-7833
経営者：(有)はますからんど
従業員：7人(うちパート3人)
客単価：600円
主なメニューと単価：パン各種100〜 ソフトクリーム250 クリームカプチーノ450 コーヒー350 雑貨200〜
*主な仕上げ材料
屋根：コンパネ下地カラーステンレス
外壁：不燃木塗装仕上げ 一部リシン吹き付け
外部柱：鉄骨組みOP半ツヤ塗装
床：米松ウレタン塗装
壁：PBt12.5ビニルクロス貼り 一部木製化粧パネル貼り
天井：木製化粧パネル貼り 一部OP
家具・什器：米松OSCL
*商店建築'98-12月号掲載

● シナモ (20P)
所在地：京都府京都市中京区寺町通二条下ル妙満寺前町454-3
工事種別：内装のみ 全面改装
床面積：105.4rm²(うち厨房6.02m²)
工期：1999年3月25日〜4月9日
*営業内容
開店：1999年4月15日
営業時間：午前11時〜午後11時
定休日：第1, 第3月曜
電話：(075)223-3969
経営者：シナモ
従業員：サービス3人 厨房2人 合計5人(うちパート2人)
客席数：26席 客単価：1500円
客回転数：3回
主な取り扱い商品＆メニューと単価：雑貨／ペーパーホルダー980 フラワーベース8500 グラス1000〜2000 キッチン用品300 カフェ／コーヒー450 ワイン(グラス)600 ランチ1000 パスタ800
*主な仕上げ材料
床：ビニルタイル貼り
壁：クロス貼り 一部ミラー貼り
天井：クロス貼り
家具：カウンター天板／杉板t30
什器：棚板／杉板t30
照明器具：オリジナルスタンド
*商店建築'99-10月号掲載

● カトル (22P)
所在地：愛知県名古屋市中村区名駅1-1-4 JRセントラルタワーズ12階
工事種別：内装のみ 新築
床面積：323.23m²(うち厨房35.16m²)
工期：1999年8月15日〜2000年2月15日
*営業内容
開店：2000年3月11日
営業時間：午前11時〜午後11時
定休日：なし 電話：(052)562-1517
経営者：ジェイアールセントラルビル(株)
運営委託：(株)トリコロール
従業員：サービス12人 厨房5人 合計17人(うちパート15人)
客席数：82席 客単価：850円
客回転数：3回
主なメニューと単価：コーヒー500 ビール600 カクテル700 ランチ950 グルメバーガー800〜 サンドイッチ800〜 ケーキセット900
主なサービスと料金：年会費3000円 インターネット30分300円 DVD 1時間400円
*主な仕上げ材料
床：黒檀フローリング
幅木：木下地染色CL仕上げ
壁：PB下地AEP ファサード／PB下地樹脂系薄塗り材左官仕上げ バー／ガラスタイル貼り
天井：スケルトン アルミルーバー吊り焼き付け塗装
家具：カバ桜染色ウレタン仕上げ 柱まわり本棚／カバ桜染色仕上げ スダレ ブルーガラス張り 壁面本棚／スチールパイプ組み透明ガラスt6透明ブルーシート貼り FL内照式
*商店建築'00-6月号掲載

● クレイトンズ (24P)
所在地：東京都港区六本木13-12-6 大昌ビル1,2階
工事種別：内外装 全面改装
床面積：1階122.96m²(うち厨房20.

04m²) 2階182.05m²(うち厨房11.36m²) 合計305.01m²
工期：2000年1月15日～3月19日
＊営業内容
開店：2000年3月27日
営業時間：月～土曜／午前7時～午前4時30分 日曜・祝日／午前9時～午後9時
定休日：なし 電話：(03)5772-7715
経営者：UCC上島珈琲(株)
従業員：社員7人 パート53人 合計60人
客席数：1階34席(スタンディング含む) 2階85席 合計119席
主なメニューと単価：1階／アイスコーヒー(180ml)280 スペシャリティーカプチーノ(270ml)300 ソフト&ライト(180ml)280 2階／クレイトンブルーマウンテン450 マイスターソフト&ライト400
＊主な仕上げ材料
床：樹脂タイル貼り
壁・天井：化粧不燃パネル(ブビンガ材練り付け染色CL二分ツヤ)目透かし貼り
家具：造作・収納／ブビンガ材柾目練り付け染色ポリウレタンクリア塗装二分ツヤ 1階カウンター／腰・鋼板メラミン焼き付け塗装 トップ・メラミン化粧板貼り 2階カウンター／腰・大理石貼りt20本磨き トップ・大理石貼りt40本磨き
＊商店建築'00-06月号掲載

● アシュビィズ オブ ロンドン 赤坂 (26P)
所在地：東京都港区赤坂3-8-8 赤坂フローラルビル1階
工事種別：内外装 全面改装
床面積：112m²(うち厨房17m²)
工期：1999年4月28日～5月21日
総工費：3370万円
＊営業内容
開店：1999年5月28日
営業時間：午前8時～午後9時 土曜・日曜・祝日／午前10時～午後8時
定休日：なし 電話：(03)3582-3571
従業員：サービス2人 厨房8人 合計10人(うちパート8人)
客席数：48席 客単価：470円
客回転数：10回
主なメニューと単価：アッサム280 ダージリン300 アールグレー280 スコーン500 シフォンケーキ520
＊主な仕上げ材料
床：パーケット ナラ材フローリング
壁：PBプラスター金ゴテ仕上げ 腰壁／カバ材
家具・什器：カバ材 ブナ材 カウンター／腰・カバ材 一部ガラスタイル貼り トップ・テラゾ
＊商店建築'99-10月号掲載

● 銀座あけぼの (28P)
所在地：東京都中央区銀座5-17-9 フォワービル地下1階, 1階
工事種別：内装のみ 全面改装
床面積：地下1階65.0m²(うち厨房4.7m²) 1階23.5m² 合計93.5m²
工期：2000年8月9日～9月13日
＊営業内容
開店：2000年9月15日
営業時間：午前9時～午後9時(日曜のみ午後8時まで)
定休日：なし 電話：(03)3571-0483
経営者：(株)曙 従業員：12人
客席数：10席 客単価：1500円
主な取り扱い商品と単価：白玉豆大福200 栗最中80 われけんこつ500 バーメニュー／煎茶と和菓子1000 抹茶と和菓子1000 焙じ茶と和菓子900 日本酒と和菓子1200 ビールと和菓子1200
＊主な仕上げ材料
サイン：ステンレスプレートHL枠組み 樹脂系和紙貼り 内部電飾
床：1階／既存のまま 地下1階／バー・墨入りモルタル金ゴテ仕上げ 売り場・着色モルタル(砂利入り)コテ仕上げ
壁：PBt12.5目透かし貼り下地調整材
天井：PBt12.5寒冷紗パテしごきAEP(シルバー)
家具：バーカウンター／ブビンガ材ムク板テクスチュア加工銀粉塗装
什器：商品棚／OSB練り付け染色(白)VCLつや消し
照明器具：ペンダント／スチールパイプ錆加工60角ウレタンクリアつや消し 内部ミニクリプトン球50W
＊商店建築'01-01月号掲載

● ケーキマニア (30P)
所在地：神奈川県横浜市中区新港町11 横浜ワールドポーターズ1階
工事種別：内装のみ 新築
床面積：157m²(うち厨房30.5m²)
工期：1999年6月下旬～8月下旬
＊営業内容
開店：1999年9月10日
営業時間：午前10時～午後11時
定休日：不定休 電話：(045)22-2155
経営者：(株)ファミール製菓
従業員：サービス15人 厨房5人 合計20人(うちパート15人)
客席数：66席 客単価：1100円
客回転数：3回
主なメニューと単価：ケーキ(50種)300～ パフェ850 ランチ1000 コーヒー550～ 紅茶600～
＊主な仕上げ材料
サイン：ステンレスメラミン焼き付け(内照ボックス) ステンレスパイプHL カラーアクリル
床：タイル貼り300角 一部50角
幅木：ステンレスHL
壁：PB下地コテ塗り塗装材 一部アートフレーム
天井：PB下地AEP
什器：ステンレスHL＋メラミン化粧板貼り
＊商店建築'00-06月号掲載

● ヴィザヴィ天神今泉店 (32P)
所在地：福岡県福岡市中央区今泉2-5-25 熊谷ビル1階
工事種別：内外装 全面改装
床面積：85.0m²(うち厨房11.13m²)
工期：1999年9月29日～10月29日
総工費：1915万円
＊営業内容
開店：1999年10月29日
営業時間：午前7時～午前0時
定休日：なし 電話：(092)737-2177
経営者：(株)シークス
従業員：サービス10人 厨房4人 合計14人(うちパート10人)
客席数：14
客単価：1300円(テイクアウト含む)
主なメニューと単価：ケーキ280～380 タルト350～450 ケーキセット700 コーヒー400
＊主な仕上げ材料
床：パイン材フローリング
壁：既存下地パイン材貼り 目地なしタイル貼り
天井：色粉シックイ金ゴテ仕上げ
什器：冷蔵ショーケース／パイン材貼り モザイクタイル貼り
＊商店建築'00-06月号掲載

● プルミエール (34P)
所在地：大阪府大阪市中央区日本橋1-25-23 アミスタユウ1階
工事種別：内外装 新築
床面積：58m²(うち厨房18m²)
工期：1999年3月2日～4月初旬
＊営業内審
開店：1999年4月14日
営業時間：午前8時～午後7時(祝日は午後6時)
定休日：日曜 電話：(06)6630-4300
経営者：古谷信昭
従業員：6人(うちアルバイト3人)
客席数：カウンター4席 テーブル18席 合計22席(うちテラスに8席)
客単価：800円 客回転数：3～4回
主なメニューと単価：ブレンドコーヒー400(お代わり無料) アイスコーヒーおよびアイスティー450 紅茶(フランス産)550 プチケーキ(季節感のあるフレッシュフルーツを使用)200～500
＊主な仕上げ材料
床：アピトン材フローリング貼り ワトコオイル塗布
幅木：擬レンガ積み
壁：寒冷紗パテシゴキAEPローラー塗り
天井：鉄筋コンクリートAEP吹き付け
家具：ヘム材ワトコオイル塗布
カウンターおよびテーブル：アバ材ワトコオイル
ボーダー：アルミブラッシング仕上げ
流木：ワトコオイル塗布
＊商店建築'99-10月号掲載

● ル・プティ・ブドン (36P)
所在地：東京都渋谷区鉢山町13-13 ヒルサイドウエストA棟1階
発注者：(株)アトリエ マリ
工事種別：内装のみ 新築
床面積：99m²(うち厨房15m²)
工期：1998年9月20日～11月15日
＊営業内容
開店：1998年11月26日
営業時間：午前10時～午後8時
定休日：なし 電話：(03)5457-0084
経営者：(株)アンドレ・パッション
従業員：サービス3人 厨房2人 合計5人
客席数：42席 客単価：1500円
客回転数：2.5回
主なメニューと単価：プティガトー各種300～ サンドイッチ700～ グラタン1000～ コーヒー500～
＊主な仕上げ材料
床：蛇紋岩象嵌レジンコンクリートタイル貼りt24 カーペット貼り
幅木：レジンコンクリート
壁：PBt12EP スタッコ塗装 透明ガラスt19埋め込み 石膏下地ウレタン塗装鏡面仕上げ アルミスパンドレル波形板貼り パーティション／木製フラッシュパネルウレタン塗装鏡面仕上げ
天井：PBt12スタッコ塗装
照明：スリット／スチール板加工メラミン焼き付け塗装
什器：ガラス棚／透明ガラスt19 ショーケース／ガラス部・ペアガラス曲面ペアガラスフレーム／ベース部・ステンレスバイブレーション仕上げ
＊商店建築'99-05月号掲載

● シーキューブ 芦屋店 (38P)
所在地：兵庫県芦屋市船戸町4-1 ラポルテ本館1, 2階
工事種別：内外装 全面改装
床面積：1階117m²(うち厨房55.5m²) 2階117m²(うち厨房15.6m²) 合計234m²
工期：1996年2月10日～3月25日(階段工事9月26日)
総工費：1億6280万円
＊営業内容
開店：1996年3月28日
営業時間：午前10時～午後10時
定休日：なし 電話：(0797)32-3773
経営者：(株)アンリ・シャルパンティエ
従業員：サービス3人 厨房3人 パート常ина4人 合計10人
客席数：56席
客単価：1階1800円 2階1000円
客回転数：4.5回
主なメニューと単価：1階ケーキ350～ 2階ピザ10種700～1700 パスタ10種700～1250 エスプレッソ450 コーヒー500
＊主な仕上げ材料
外壁：1階／ペアガラス(厨房部分) 透明ガラスt10Fix(ケーキショップ) 2階／ハードメープル材取り付け回転扉形式 ガラスt10Fix SC側通路／大理石貼り 一部ガラスFix
床：1階／タイル貼り300角 2階／オーク材染色フローリング貼り モザイクタイル貼り20角
壁：1階／砂岩乱貼り イタリアンスタッコ ガラスブロック190角 ハードメープル材染色ウレタン塗装
天井：1階／寒冷紗パテシゴキAEP塗装 2階／寒冷紗パテシゴキしっくい塗装
カウンター&レジカウンター：ポリエステル塗装
テーブル：天板／ラミネート板貼りUV塗装 脚／ステンレスサンドブラスト仕上げ
階段：ささら／ステンレスφ76.3×t3HL＋φ45バフ磨き 踏み板／強化ガラスt12合わせガラス トップ・タペストリー加工 トラス／ステンレスムク材磨き仕上げ＋ステンレスφ15磨き仕上げ
＊商店建築'97-04月号掲載

● フレスカ (40P)
所在地：福島県耶麻郡猪苗代町大字三ツ和字村南1224-1
工事種別：一戸建て　新築
用途地域地区：無指定
建ぺい率：制限60％＞実効18.17％
容積率：制限200％＞実効20.09％
構造と規模：S造　地上2階建て
敷地面積：1485㎡
建築面積：269.88㎡
床面積：1階264.77㎡(うち厨房12.5㎡)　2階33.6㎡　合計298.37㎡
工期：1997年3月1日～7月24日
＊営業内容
開店：1997年7月30日
営業時間：午前9時～午後6時
定休日：なし　電話：(0242)72-1101
経営者：(株)三万石
従業員：サービス3人　厨房3人　合計6人(うちアルバイト3人)
客席数：60席　客単価：900円
客回転数：2.5回
主なメニューと単価：イタリアンカフェバリエーション10種／400　オリジナルヨーグルトメニュー8種／450～600　パニーニ(イタリアンサンド)7種／600～750　ハーブピザ4種／750～850　アップルパイ／1カット400
＊主な仕上げ材料
屋根：ガルバリウム鋼板竪ハゼ葺きt0.4　ALC板t100アスファルト防水
外壁：乾式外装タイル
中庭：石英岩乱貼り
床：ラミネートタイル貼りt3.0
壁：寒冷紗パテシゴキAEP塗装　一部米松柾目板貼りt12
天井：寒冷紗パテシゴキAEP塗装
什器：チーク材ポリウレタン塗装　アルミ板生地t5
＊商店建築'98-04月号掲載

● クレーム デ ラ クレーム (43P)
所在地：京都府京都市中京区烏丸通竹屋町少将井町225
工事種別：一戸建て　新築
用途地域地区：商業地域
建ぺい率：制限100％＞実効87.48％
容積率：制限600％＞実効263.18％
構造と規模：S造　一部RC造　地下1階　地上4階建て
敷地面積：204.04㎡
建築面積：178.50㎡
店舗階床面積：1階176.38㎡　2階161.67㎡　合計338.05㎡(うち厨房83.13㎡)
工期：1999年3月18日～10月31日
＊営業内容
開店：1999年11月11日
営業時間：午前10時～午後7時(カフェ午前11時開店)
定休日：火曜　電話：(075)241-4547
経営者：(株)石田老舗
従業員：サービス9人　厨房11人　合計20人(うちパート10人)
客席数：2階42席
客単価：1階1800円　2階900円
客回転数：4回
主なメニューと単価：1階／シュークリーム(30種)180～450　デコレーションシュークリーム一台(6人前)2300～4000　2階／コーヒー450～　紅茶500～　フレッシュジュース600　シューランチ1200～1500　シューデリカ750～950
＊主な仕上げ材料
床：テラコッタ貼り500角　縁甲板フローリング貼り　長尺塩ビシート貼りt2.5
壁：珪藻土コテ仕上げ　モザイクタイル
天井：珪藻土コテ仕上げ　一部AEP塗装
＊商店建築'00-06月号掲載

● A.D.K. (46P)
所在地：東京都港区南青山5-12-3　笄兄弟社ビルヂング地下1階，1階
工事種別：内外装　全面改装
床面積：地下1階97.6㎡　1階66.97㎡　合計164.57㎡(2階厨房を除く)
工期：1998年2月9日～4月25日
＊営業内容
開店：1998年5月15日
営業時間：午前11時30分～午後2時30分　午後6時～午後8時(レストランのみ午後9時30分まで)
定休日：日曜・祝日
電話：(03)3406-6002
経営者：(株)笄兄弟社
従業員：サービス9人　厨房6人　合計15人
客席数：1階／20席　地下1階／45席
客単価：1500～2000円　客回転数：5回
主なメニューと単価：フォカッチャ380　ルーコラとプロシュートのピッツァ440　仔羊とジャガイモのロースト480(100g)　エスプレッソ200　カプチーノ280
＊主な仕上げ材料
屋根：テント張り　スチールフレーム焼き付け塗装枠
外壁：H形鋼塗装仕上げ　幅木／モルタル　腰／ガラスブロック
サイン：ステンレスフレーム　アクリルロゴシート貼り内照式
床：カバ材ムク板フローリング　ストライプ貼りクリア　一部石英岩貼り
壁：既存のまま
天井：PB下地AEP
家具・什器：カバ材突き板柾目染色CL仕上げ
＊商店建築'98-12月号掲載

● ニューヨークデリ (48P)
所在地：大阪府大阪市中央区南船場4長堀地下街7号
工事種別：内装のみ　新築
床面積：114㎡(うち厨房23.6㎡)
工期：1997年2月1日～4月30日
＊営業内容
開店：1997年5月21日
営業時間：午前7時30分～午後10時
定休日：第2水曜
電話：(06)6282-2188
経営者：(株)アサヒディード
従業員：サービス2人　厨房2人　パート6人　合計10人
客席数：36席　客単価：850円
客単価：8回
主なメニューと単価：デリカテッセン(シングル)200～500　サンドイッチ350～550　ビール500～　ワイン350～550
＊主な仕上げ材料
床：客席／フローリング貼りt15
壁：客席／モザイクタイル貼り19角
厨房／タイル貼り100角
天井：寒冷紗パテシゴキAEP
家具：桜材ムク染色
什器：キッチンカウンター／ステンレス
＊商店建築'98-12月号掲載

● 632 (50P)
所在地：東京都渋谷区神宮前6-32-10
工事種別：一戸建て　新築
用途地域地区：第二種中高層住居専用地域
建ぺい率：制限70％＞実効68.52％
容積率：制限300％＞実効134.37％
構造と規模：S造　地上2階　塔屋1階建て
敷地面積：518.50㎡
建築面積：355.32㎡
床面積：1階(店舗)352.98㎡　2階327.84㎡　塔屋15.91㎡　合計696.73㎡(うち厨房68.17㎡)
工期：1999年1月12日～4月25日
総工費：1億8924.8万円
＊営業内容
開店：1999年5月28日
営業時間：午前8時～午前0時(日曜・祝日は午後10時まで)
定休日：なし　電話：(03)3498-0632
経営者：ピアザフーズシステム(株)
従業員：サービス29人　厨房13人　合計42人(うちパート29人)
客席数：115席　客単価：1200円
客回転数：5.5回
主なメニューと単価：マグロのタルタル950　クラムチャウダー480　キノコぞうすい750　632Tボーンステーキ6320　スパークリングワイン600　コーヒー280
＊主な仕上げ材料
屋根：折板t0.8　カラー鋼板
外壁：角波サイディングカラー鋼板　コンクリート打ち放し樹脂系複層仕上げ材
床：イペ材フローリングOF
壁：樹脂系複層仕上げ材
天井：PBt12.5AEP　デッキプレート素地貼り
家具：イス・テーブル／ステンレスエンボス仕上げ　スチール亜鉛メッキ仕上げ
什器：ステンレスバイブレーション仕上げ　ブナ材突き板CL
階段手摺り：ステンレスHL仕上げ＋エキスパンドメタルシルバー塗装
＊商店建築'99-10月号掲載

● キャスロン (52P)
所在地：宮城県仙台市泉区紫山1-4　泉パークタウン紫山プラザ
工事種別：一戸建て　新築
用途地域地区：近隣商業地域
建ぺい率：制限60％＞実効4.22％
容積率：制限200％＞実効4.13％
構造と規模：S造　平屋建て
敷地面積：6606㎡
建築面積：278.93㎡
床面積：272.93㎡(うち厨房67.14㎡)
工期：1999年3月15日～7月2日
＊営業内容
開店：1999年7月24日
営業時間：午前10時～午後9時
定休日：なし　電話：(022)377-8891
経営者：(株)キャスロン
従業員：サービス30人　ベーカリー10人　合計40人(うちパート34人)
客単価：カフェ1000円　物販3000円　ベーカリー600円
客回転数：6回
主なメニューと単価：カフェ／エスプレッソ300　ダージリンティー600　ピザ1200～　サンドイッチ800　ベーカリー／天然酵母パン1斤300　フランスパン300　プロダクト／マグカップ2000　タンブラーS1200　M1400
主な仕上げ材料
屋根：ALC板シート防水
外壁：セメント系外壁材コテ仕上げ
サイン：スチール板メラミン焼き付け塗装
床：タイル貼り275角
壁：PBt125生石灰クリームローラー仕上げ
天井：PBt9.5EP
家具・什器：カフェサービスカウンター／甲板・人造大理石　腰・OSB板染色CLツヤ消し
ディスプレイステージ／甲板・人造大理石　開き戸・メラミン化粧板貼り
＊商店建築'00-06月号掲載

● パン・ド・ケルシー (54P)
所在地：群馬県高崎市上小塙町849
工事種別：一戸建て　新築
用途地域地区：都市計画区域内
建ぺい率：制限70％＞実効18.90％
容積率：制限400％＞実効18.90％
構造と規模：木造　平屋建て
敷地面積：1659.00㎡
建築面積：313,65㎡
床面積：313.65㎡(うち厨房95.51㎡)
工期：1998年4月20日～8月31日
総工費：1億1500万円
＊営業内容
開店：1998年9月19日
営業時間：午前11時～午後10時(ベーカリー／午前8時～午後9時)
定休日：なし　電話：(027)360-4855
経営者：(株)フーケ
従業員：50人(うちアルバイト35人)
客単価：1000円
主なメニューと単価：スパゲティトマトソース730　スパゲティランチ980～1180　グラスワイン500　コーヒー400
＊主な仕上げ材料
屋根：ガルバリウム鋼板t0.6　ルーフデッキ(シルバー)
外壁：モルタル刷毛引き塗りリシン特注色吹き付け
床：フローリング　テラコッタタイル貼り300角　パティオ／ウッドデッキ
壁：PB下地AEPツヤ消し塗装
天井：PB下地銘木突き板貼りCL　AEPツヤ消し塗装
家具・什器：ブナ材突き板CL　天然木ボード
＊商店建築'98-12月号掲載

第2章　カフェ&ティールーム

● 櫻茶屋 (58P)
所在地：徳島県徳島市北沖洲3-8-61
工事種別：一戸建て　全面改装
用途地域地区：準工業地域
建ぺい率：制限60％＞実効56.65％
容積率：制限200％＞実効76.31％
構造と規模：S造　地上2階建て
敷地面積：887.54m²
建築面積：502.86m²
床面積：店舗369.67m²(うち厨房151.75m²)
工期：1996年6月8日～11月30日
総工費：9150万円
＊営業内容
開店：1996年12月7日
営業時間：午前9時30分～午後10時
定休日：なし　電話：(0886)64-1251
経営者：(有)吉田海産
従業員：サービス1人　厨房2人
パート4人　合計7人
客席数：64席　客単価：800円
客回転数：5回
主なメニューと単価：櫻ブレンド480
紅茶500　自家製パン400　櫻カレー1000　ランチセット800
＊主な仕上げ材料
屋根：既存ルーフ塗り替え
外壁：擬レンガタイル貼り　ジュラク風塗材塗布
外部床：駐車場／砂利および木埋め込みアスファルト　アプローチ／サビ御影石貼り
サイン：ボンデ鋼板t2.3ウレタン塗装
床：フローリング
壁：擬レンガタイル貼り　スクリーン／ガラスエッチング加工　スチールフレームt10サビ仕上げ
天井：野地板／米松材染色CL
家具：カウンター／米松集成材
什器：米松集成材染色ポリウレタン仕上げ　ブビンガ材ポリウレタン仕上げ
＊商店建築'97-07月号掲載

● ネスカフェ (61P)
所在地：兵庫県神戸市中央区御幸通り7-1-15
工事種別：内外装　新築
床面積：1階75.74m²　2階72.10m²
合計147.84m²(うち厨房10.44m²)
工期：1999年7月中旬～9月下旬
＊営業内容
開店：1999年10月1日
営業時間：平日／午前10時～午後8時
土曜・日曜・祝日／午前11時～午後8時
定休日：なし　電話：(078)230-7098
経営者：ネスレ日本(株)
運営委託：ホテルオークラ神戸
従業員：サービス4人　厨房6人
合計10人
客席数：1階25席　2階35席　テラス席32席　合計92席
主なメニューと単価：カフェオレバニラ300　カフェラッテラズベリー300
カプチーノ280　サンドイッチ380～480　ネスカフェクッキー160
＊主な仕上げ材料
屋根：キーストンプレートt1.2下地アルミt2

ファサード：フロート板ガラスt19カーテンウォール
床：磁器質タイル貼り　一部ガラスモザイクタイル貼り
壁：PBt12.5AEPステンレス目地入り　一部繊維混入石膏板t9二重貼り
天井：PBt12.5AEP
家具：ステンレス磨き　スチールクロムメッキ　ビニルレザー張り
什器：カウンタートップ／大理石
＊商店建築'00-06月号掲載

● ロッジ (64P)
所在地：静岡県沼津市江原町4-13
工事種別：一戸建て　新築
用途地域地区：第一種住居専用地域
建ぺい率：制限60％＞実効5.3％
容積率：制限200％＞実効8.1％
構造と規模：木造　地上2階建て
敷地面積：656.09m²
建築面積：34.67m²
床面積：1階34.67m²　2階18.50m²
合計53.17m²(うち厨房面積10.00m²)
工期：2000年4月1日～7月14日
総工費：1050万円
＊営業内容
開店：2000年7月19日
営業時間：午前9時30分～午後10時
定休日：月曜、火曜
電話：(0559)23-4070
経営者：川村富士雄　川村幸子
従業員：サービス1人　厨房1人
合計2人
客席数：16席　客単価：700円
客回転数：6回
主なメニューと単価：ブレンドコーヒー400　カフェラテ600　紅茶400
ピザ700　ハヤシライス600　サンドイッチ500
＊主な仕上げ付料
屋根：ガルバリウム鋼板t0.35瓦棒葺き
外壁：ステンレスt0.4HL　硬質木毛セメント板t12EP
床：コンクリート金ゴテ下地塗り床仕上
壁：押し出し中空セメント板t15撥水剤塗布　PBt12.5EP
家具：壁面収納／MDF板ウレタンクリア　カウンター／人造大理石　テーブル／メラミンソリッド材貼り　ステンレス角パイプ　ベンチ／外部用ビニルレザー張り　ステンレス角パイプ
＊商店建築'01-01月号掲載

● 珈琲クラブ (66P)
所在地：香川県高松市多肥下町737-1
工事種別：一戸建て　新築
用途地域地区：第二種住居地域
建ぺい率：制限60％＞実効11.61％
容積率：制限200％＞実効11.41％
構造と規模：木造　平屋建て
敷地面積：538.59m²
建築面積：62.49m²
床面積：61.45m²
工期：1999年2月4日～4月20日
＊営業内容
開店：1999年4月30日
営業時間：午前9時一午後8時
定休日：なし　電話：(087)867-3599
経営者：梁先克武
従業貞：サービス6人　厨房2人

合計8人(うちパート6人)
客席数：29席　客単価：700円
客回転数：5.5回
主なメニューと単価：ハウスブレンド500　炭焼きブレンド500　カプチーノ600　カフェ・ラテ600　フレンチトースト600
＊主な仕上げ材料
屋根：カラー鋼板葺き
外壁：サイディングt12樹脂系薄塗り材
塀：ぐり石積み上げ貼り　一部杉板貼り防腐塗装
外部柱：杉板105角木材保護着色塗装
サイン：アクリル板t5シート文字貼り　石積みの上真鍮板エッチング文字入り
床：アピトン材t12貼りOSウレタン塗装
幅木：アピトン材OSウレタン塗装
壁：珪藻土寒冷紗貼り　一部掻き落とし
天井：ビニルクロス貼り
テーブル・カウンター：ブビンガ材OSポリウレタン塗装
建具：ブビンガ材単板貼りOSウレタン塗装
＊商店建築'00-06月号掲載

● ミケランジェロ (68P)
所在地：東京都渋谷区猿楽町35-1
工事種別：一戸建て　新築
床面積：114m²(うち厨房15m²)
工期：1997年3月1日～6月10日
総工費：8420万円
＊営業内容
開店：1997年6月20日
営業時間：午前11時～午前0時
定休日：なし　電話：(03)3770-9517
経営者：(株)ひらまつ
従業員：30人(うちアルバイト24人)
客席数：140席　客単価：1000円
客回転数：5回
主なメニューと単価：コーヒー600
エスプレッソ400　カプチーノ600
オリジナルハーブティー600　トスカーナ風パンと野菜のサラダ600
＊主な仕上げ材料
屋根：鉄骨組み網入りクリアペアガラス
外壁：ガラスブロック　スチール建具
壁：ガラスブロック　スチール建具
天井：網入りクリアペアガラス　可動式
家具・什器：木製(特注品)
照明器具：特注ペンダント
＊商店建築'98-04月号掲載

● カフェ・ド・フロール (70P)
所在地：東京都渋谷区神宮前5-1-2
工事種別：一戸建て　全面改装
床面積：120m²(うち厨房15m²)
＊営業内容
開店：1995年12月2日
営業時間：午前10時～午後11時30分
定休日：なし　電話：(03)3406-8805
経営者：粧美堂(株)
従業員：サービス5人　厨房4人
合計9人
客席数：88席　客単価：1000円
月商目標：2000万円
客回転数：6.5回
＊主なメニューと単価：エスプレッソコーヒー600　カフェ・オレ850　クラブサンドイッチ1200
＊主な仕上げ材料

屋根：折板ルーフィング
外壁：セラミックボード下地エマルション系吹き付け塗材塗布
床：特注モザイクタイル貼り
幅木：マホガニー材OS染色
壁：PBt12AEPローラー仕上げ　腰部／マホガニー材OS染色
照明器具：特注(フランス製、20年代のクリスタルガラス再現製作)
家具：特注籐製チェア　メラミン樹脂製天板カフェテーブル(すべてフランス製)
折り畳み戸：スチール製エッチングガラスFix
＊商店建築'96-06月号掲載

● フォート マックヘンリー (72P)
所在地：東京都渋谷区恵比寿1-7-12
久保ビル地下1階
工事種別：内装のみ　新築
床面積：45m²(うち厨房6m²)
工期：1995年3月29日～4月20日
総工費：800万円
＊営業内容
開店：1995年4月26日
営業時間：午前8時～午後11時
定休日：なし　電話：(03)3473-0885
経営者：(株)ハイブリッジ・プランニング
従業員：サービス・厨房　合計2人
客席数：25席　客単価：650円
客回転数：2.5回
主なメニューと単価：カフェラテ450
ケーキ600　フレーバーコーヒー500
サンドウィッチ500～
＊主な仕上げ材料
サイン：米松板目白染色CL
床：パイン材フローリングワックス塗装
壁：コンクリート下地土壁風仕上げ
天井：スケルトン
照明：スポットライト　特注ガラスペンダント
家具：パイン材ワックス仕上げ
パーティション＆カウンター：スチール亜鉛メッキ仕上げ
＊商店建築'95-10月号掲載

● 鈴木 (74P)
所在地：神奈川県厚木市中町3-5-6
ロックヒルズ本厚木駅前101
工事種別：内外装　全面改装
床面積：31m²(うち厨房3.4m²)
工期：1999年7月6日～10月6日
＊営業内容
開店：1999年10月11日
営業時間：午後1時～午前0時
定休日：火曜　電話：(046)295-6280
経営者：鈴木直治
従業員：サービス3人　厨房2人
合計5人(うちパート3人)
客席数：18席　客単価：800円
客回転数：4回
主なメニューと単価：自家焙煎コーヒー／エスプレッソ750　カプチーノ750　カフェモカ・カフェラテ750
コーヒーゼリー800　コーヒー＋ケーキ1000
＊主な仕上げ材料
外壁：腐食鋼板t1.5
入り口引き戸／ブビンガ材ムク拭き漆仕上げ　ガラス窓／カラードアンティ

データ内容は月刊商店建築掲載時のものです

ーク
床：珪藻土タタキ黒染め
壁：よしずの上И漆和紙張り　腐食銅板t1.0　腰／黒御影石JB
天井：腐食銅板t1.0
家具：カウンター／ブビンガ材ムク拭き漆仕上げ
＊商店建築'00-06月号掲載

● ショパン (77P)
所在地：大阪府枚方市川原町13-20 第2クラウンマンション1階
工事種別：内外装　新築
床面積：77.88m²(うち厨房11.52m²)
工期：1996年11月7日〜12月6日
＊営業内容
開店：1996年12月14日
営業時間：午前7時〜午後8時
定休日：水曜　電話：(0720)46-5222
経営者：楮谷尚夫
従業員：サービス1人　厨房1人　パート常時1人　合計3人
客席数：37席　客単価：400円
客回転数：2.5回
主なメニューと単価：コーヒー・紅茶350　モーニングセット350〜450　カレー600　日替わりランチ700
＊主な仕上げ材料
サイン：アクリル乳半ボックスカッティングシート貼り
床：タイル貼り100角
壁：P8t12EP　桜材単板練り付け染色CL
天井：PBt12EP
照明ボックス：特注布貼りアクリル
＊商店建築'97-04月号掲載

● ムジカ・ラ・ラ (80P)
所在地：京都府京都市下京区烏丸通り塩小路下ル JR京都ビル7階東広場
工事種別：内装のみ　新築
床面積：85.47m²(うち厨房18.76m²)
工期：1996年12月20日〜1997年7月14日
＊営業内容
開店：1997年9月11日
営業時間：午前10時〜午後11時
定休日：なし　電話：(075)385-3385
経営者：(株)シアターアーツ1200
従業員：サービス5人　厨房2人　合計7人
客席数：49席　客単価：800円
客回転：13回
主なメニューと単価：カフェ(ムジカブレンド)450　キャラメルミルクティー700　ケーキ＆ジェラート700　チキンディアブロサンド700　オリジナルカクテル800〜
＊主な仕上げ材料
床：せっ器質タイル貼り310角
壁：磁器質タイル貼り200角　PBt12AEP塗装
天井：繊維混入石膏板EP
テーブル：天板／ポリエステル系人造石
カウンター：天板／ナラ材ウレタンクリア　腰／スチール板シルバーメタリック塗装
＊商店建築'98-04月号掲載

● シネマカフェ (82P)
所在地：東京都立川市曙町2-8-5

シネマシティ1階
工事種別：内装のみ　新築
床面積：165m²(うち厨房16.7m²)
工期：1998年7月10日〜8月22日
＊営業内容
開店：1998年8月31日
営業時間：午前11時〜午後10時
定休日：なし　電話：(042)527-7721
経営者：シネマシティ(株)
従業員：サービス15人　厨房2人　合計17人(うちパート15人)
客席数：66席　客単価：480円
客回転数：6回
主なメニューと単価：ローストチキンサンド650　パウンドケーキ280　ブレンドコーヒー350　エスプレッソ350　カフェラテ400
＊主な仕上げ材料
外壁：スチールフッ素焼き付け塗装　クリアガラスt8FIX
サイン：PBt12.5AEPの上ロゴマークシルク印刷
床：モルタル金ゴテOP
壁：PBt12.5AEP　カラーアクリル貼りt5　柱／古材貼り
天井：ケイカル板AEP
家具：カウンター／トップ・木下地ステンレス鏡面仕上げ　腰／シナ合板ラッカー塗装
＊商店建築'98-12月号掲載

● ケニア (84P)
所在地：滋賀県大津市浜町2-1 浜大津アーカス・アミューズメント館2階
工事種別：内装のみ　新築
床面積：102m²(うち厨房25m²)
工期：1998年3月21日〜4月10日
＊営業内容
開店：1998年4月23日
営業時間：午前10時〜午後10時
定休日：なし　電話：(077)523-7055
経営者：奥田正之
従業員：8人(うちパート3人)
客席数：44席　客単価：650円
客回転数：3回
主なメニューと単価：オリジナルブレンド400　エスプレッソ400　カフェラテ400　イタリアンフローズンドリンク(グラニータ)500　生ハムのミラノ風サンド900
＊主な仕上げ材料
床：人造大理石貼り　樺桜材フローリング染色クリアウレタン　一部ステンレスサテンプレートt1.5
幅木：木製ラッカー塗装　樺桜材染色クリアウレタン　H60
壁：PBt12.5AEPおよび不燃突き板染色CL
家具：ビッグテーブル＆テーブル／トップ・樺桜染色UV仕上げ
什器：レジ台／バーズアイメープル染色クリアウレタン　カウンター／ステンレスサテンプレートt1.5
＊商店建築'98-12月号掲載

● シャノアール両国店 (86P)
所在地：東京都墨田区両国2-21-2 両国ダイカンプラザ2階
工事種別：内装のみ　全面改装
床面積：300m²(うち厨房15m²)
工期：1997年10月25日〜12月8日

＊営業内容
開店：1997年12月9日
営業時間：午前7時〜午後11時
定休日：なし　電話：(03)3632-7198
経営者：(株)シャノアール
従業員数：サービス20人　厨房10人　合計30人(うちアルバイト27人)
客席数：145席　客単価：423円
客回転数：4.8回
主なメニューと単価：ブレンドコーヒー280　エスプレッソ300　カフェオレ330　ケーキセット680　朝食セット360〜460　ケーキ360〜
＊主な仕上げ材料
床：強化リノリウムパターン貼り
幅木：鉄板メラミン焼き付け塗装H75
壁：PBt12.5EP系吹き付け塗材　モルタル掻き落とし　ウォールナット材およびオーク材突き板練り付け　パーティション／鍛鉄ウレタン仕上げ
天井：PBt12.5AEP
家具：テーブル／天板・ウォールナット材OS　脚・鍛鉄ウレタン仕上げ　イス／座・革紐編み仕上げ　脚・鍛鉄ウレタン仕上げ
＊商店建築'98-12月号掲載

● クレシェンテ (88P)
所在地：東京都立川市柴崎町3-4-17 岡部ビル1階
工事種別：内装のみ　新築
床面積：59.7m²(うち厨房18.7m²)
工期：1999年6月30日〜8月5日
＊営業内容
開店：1999年8月11日
経営者：(有)岡部果実店
営業時間：午前7時30分〜午後8時
日躍：午前8時〜午後7時
定休日：水曜　電話：(042)524-9180
客単価：380円　席数：36席
＊主なメニューと単価：ブレンドコーヒー150　エスプレッソ200　カプチーノ250　パニーニ(バジル＆チキン)350
＊主な仕上げ材料
床：大理石貼り　一部黒御影石バーナー仕上げパターン貼り
壁・天井：PBt12.5特殊塗装　突き板染色ウレタン　ステンレスHLt5目地貼り　壁面一部リブ材貼りパネル＋スリットライト(カラーアクリル内照式)
什器：メーンカウンター／ステンレスHLφ15くり抜き加工＋乳半アクリル内照式　光りカウンター／乳半アクリルt5曲げ加工内照式
照明：オブジェ照明／乳半アクリルボックス積み200×200角
＊商店建築'00-06月号掲載

● ノア (90P)
所在地：東京都中央区銀座5-8-5 銀座5丁目ビル地下1階
工事種別：内外装　全面改装
床面積：165m²(うち厨房11m²)
工期：1998年3月29日〜5月7日
＊営業内容
開店：1998年5月9日
営業時間：午前8時〜午後11時
定休日：なし　電話：(03)3574-8324
経営者：(株)ノア

従業員：サービス8人　厨房4人　合計12人(うちパート6人)
客席数：90席　客単価：750円
客回転数：6回
主なメニューと単価：モーニングサービス480　パニーニセット750　ドリップコーヒー480　エスプレッソ550　カプチーノ600　ケーキ500〜
＊主な仕上げ材料
アプローチ：床／白御影石バーナー仕上げ　壁／スチールプレート焼き付け塗装　庇／ステンレスプレート焼き付け塗装
床：カリン材フローリング染色ウレタン仕上げ　大理石貼り
壁：寒冷紗総パテAEP　通路／アルミスパンドレル焼き付け型エナメル塗装　スクリーン／スチールFB枠　スチールプレートパターン抜き焼き付け塗装　壁面照明オブジェ／アルミプレートt8エナメル塗装
天井：寒冷紗総パテAEP　上がり天井／アクリル乳半和紙貼り　フレーム・スチールFB焼き付け塗装
家具・什器：テーブル／ブビンガ単板染色クリアウレタン仕上げ　ステンレスフレーム大理石貼り　ソファ／スエード調合成皮革　張り分け
＊商店建築'98-12月号掲載

● タカノ フルーツパーラー ＆フルーツバー (93P)
所在地：東京都新宿区新宿3-37-12 新宿ノワ2階(現存せず)
工事種別：内装のみ　新築
床面積：473.75m²(うち厨房86m²)
工期：1998年8月上旬〜9月30日
＊営業内容
開店：1998年10月10日
営業時間：パーラー／午前10時30分〜午後10時　フルーツバー／午前11時〜午後10時30分
経営者：(株)タカノフルーツパーラー
従業員：サービス22人　厨房18人　合計40人(うちパート20人)
客席数：パーラー54席　フルーツバー76席　合計130席
主なメニューと単価：パーラー／フルーツパフェ950　フルーツみつ豆900　フルーツバー(バイキング90分)／ランチタイム2000　デザートタイム3000　ディナータイム3000
＊主な仕上げ材料
床：カリン材フローリングの上ウレタンクリアツヤ消しW150　セラミックタイル貼り600角　アクリル入り特注テラゾタイル貼り150角　白大理石貼り400角
壁：特注レリーフの上AEP　ライムストーン貼り本磨き仕上げ　光り柱／網入りガラスt6.8　塗り壁仕上げ
天井：PB12.5AEP塗装
家具：テーブル／天板・レース入り合わせガラス　人造大理石
照明器具：テーブルスタンド／特注アクリルシェード
＊商店建築'98-12月号掲載

● ジュースプラス (96P)
所在地：東京都新宿区新宿3-14-1 新宿伊勢丹本館2階

153

工事種別：内装のみ　全面改装
床面積：115.55m²(うち厨房28.36m²)
工期：1998年8月1日～21日
総工費：1803万円
＊営業内容
開店：1998年8月28日
営業時間：午前10時～午後7時30分
定休日：水曜　電話：(03)3352-1111
経営者：長谷観光(株)
従業員：サービス17人　厨房4人
合計21人(うちパート14人)
客席数：72席　客単価：850円
客回転数：2.5～4回
主なメニューと単価：ひよこ豆のカレー1100　フォカッチャサンド650～　オリジナルフレッシュジュース700
＊主な仕上げ材料
床：塩ビタイル貼り　長尺ビニルシート貼り
壁：PBt12.5AEP　アクリル透明ディスプレイボックスおよびアクリル気泡入り棒取り付け
天井：PBt12.5AEP
家具・什器：イス／透明アクリル　ベンチ／ビニルレザー張り　レジ台・バック棚・吊り戸棚・サービス台／メラミン化粧板練り付け
＊商店建築'99-10月号掲載

● e-ストリートベーグルズ虎ノ門 (98P)
所在地：東京都港区西新橋1-23-9
工事種別：内外装　部分改装
床面積：70m²(うち厨房27m²)
工期：1998年3月2日～4月1日
＊営業内容
開店：1998年4月20日
営業時間：午前8時～午後8時
定休日：土曜・日曜・祝日
電話：(03)5521-1361
経営者：(株)イー・ストリート・ベーグルズ
従業員：サービス7人　厨房5人
合計12人(うちパート7人)
客席数：26席　客単価：800円
客回転数：9回
主なメニューと単価：ベーグル(10種)150　クリームチーズ(8種)130　アイスコーヒー280　カプチーノ320
＊主な仕上げ材料
サイン：ボンデ鋼板チャンネル文字メラミン焼き付け塗装
床：樹脂タイル貼り
壁・天井：PB下地AEP
什器：カウンター／天板・ステンレス　腰・チップボード
＊商店建築'98-12月号掲載

● レガーロ 虎ノ門店 (100P)
所在地：東京都港区虎ノ門1-22-13
秋山ビル1階
工事種別：内外装　全面改装
床面積：174m²(うち厨房31.3m²)
＊営業内容
開店：1995年11月7日
営業時間：午前7時30分～午後11時
定休日：日曜・祝日
電話：(03)3597-0058
経営者：(株)イエス・ワン
従業員：12人(うちパート3～4人)
客席数：80席　客単価：450円

月商目標：500万円
客回転数：5～7回
主なメニューと単価：コーヒー250　メンチカツサンド290　肉じゃがコロッケサンド270
＊主な仕上げ材料
床：塩ビタイル貼り
幅木：メープル材染色CL
壁・天井：PBt12.5AEPローラー仕上げ
家具：メラミン化粧板貼り
回り縁：カッティングシートにシルク印刷
その他：メニューボード／シナ合板黒板塗装仕上げ　カッティングシート
＊商店建築'96-06月号掲載

● グリーン (102P)
所在地：東京都港区南麻布4-1-29
広尾ガーデン2階
工事種別：内装のみ　全面改装
床面積：49.3m²(うち厨房10.6m²)
工期：1995年4月3日～27日
＊営業内容
開店：1995年4月29日
営業時間：午前11時～午後9時
定休日：第2・3火曜
電話：(03)3442-1851
経営者：(株)中央亭
従乗員：2人　客席数：24席
主なメニューと単価：ケーキ各種350　ティーセット800　ハンバーガー550　コーヒー・紅茶各500
＊主な仕上げ材料
サイン：スチール焼き付け塗装
床：大理石貼り
壁：ボード塗装　一部ミラーストライプ貼り　壁面グラフィックパネル貼り
天井：ボード塗装
照明器具：吊り照明／特注
什器：テーブル／甲板・人造大理石貼り　冷蔵ケース付きカウンター／人造大理石貼り　天井吊りプランター／スチール角パイプパンチング
＊商店建築'95-10月号掲載

● 嵐山 宇治庵 (104P)
所在地：千葉県千葉市おゆみ野3-96-4 (現存せず)
工事種別：内外装　全面改装
床面積：89m²(うち厨房23m²)
工期：2000年2月8日～3月7日
＊営業内容
開店：2000年3月17日
営業時間：午前10時～午後5時30分
定休日：土曜・日曜
経営者：(有)千葉総合企画
従業員：サービス2人　厨房4人(うちパート2人)
客席数：35席　客単価：950～1100円
客回転数：5回
主なメニューと単価：ランチ／900・980・1300　おでん600　おぞうに500　宇治パフェー700　おはぎ250
＊主な仕上げ材料
外壁：ALC板OP塗装＋クリアアクリルt10タペストリーシート貼り
サイン：樹脂シートデザイン貼り
床：塩ビタイル貼り
壁：和紙貼り　一部間接照明パネル／特殊和紙貼り
天井：PB下地AEP塗装　一部造作＆下がり天井／和紙貼り

家具：イス／合成皮革レザー　テーブル／いぐさ貼り　強化ガラス三枚重ねt30　人工植栽ディスプレイ
照明器具：オリジナル竹コードペンダント
＊商店建築'01-01号掲載

● 茶語 (106P)
所在地：東京都港区北青山2-14-6
青山ベルコモンズ5階
工事種別：内装のみ　全面改装
床面積：56.89m²(うち厨房16.33m²)
工期：2000年10月10日～30日
＊営業内容
開店：2000年11月9日
営業時間：午前11時30分～午後10時30分
定休日：不定　電話：(03)3475-8055
経営者：日本緑茶センター(株)
従業員：サービス9人　厨房5人
合計14人(うちパート12人)
客席数：26席　客単価：1300円
客回転数：6回
主なメニューと単価：龍井茶葉カレー1000　江南省産信陽毛尖(バランスの良い緑茶)800　福建省産黄金桂(甘みと香りが特徴の青茶)700　広西省産桂花茶(桂花キンモクセイと緑茶をブレンドした花茶)700
＊主な仕上げ材
床：客席／ハードメープル材フローリング　アプローチ／ライムストーン貼り
壁：PBt12.5左官仕上げ　AEP　一部モルタル　スチール格子
天井：PBt12.5AEP
家具・什器：シオジ材柾目CL
＊商店建築'01-01月号掲載

● ラウンジ235 (108P)
所在地：京都府京都市中京区六角通東洞院西入ル堂之前町
頂法寺会館本館1階
工事種別：一戸建て　増改築
床面積：242.09m²(うち厨房24.79m²)
工期：1994年10月1日～1996年10月31日
＊営業内容
開店：1997年1月16日
営業時間：午前8時～午後6時
定休日：土曜・日曜
電話：(075)221-2686
経営者：池坊　従業員：6人
客席数：60席　客回転数：2回
主なメニューと単価：コーヒー250　紅茶250～300　ソフトドリンク300～400　トースト200　サンドイッチ500　池坊関係者と同伴のみ利用可
＊主な仕上げ材料
床：大理石t25本磨き仕上げ　フェルト下地カーペット敷きt12
幅木：大理石t25本磨き仕上げ　H100
壁：陶器質仕上げ塗材　大理石t25本磨き仕上げ
天井：PBt9.5二重貼りAEP　GRG成形材下地アルミ箔チップ吹き付け塗装
家具・什器：特注ソファ、特注ガラステーブル
照明器具：色ガラス壁面埋め込み　ユニバーサルダウンライト
＊商店建築'97-04月号掲載

第3章　カフェ レストラン

● リコルディ (112P)
所在地：京都府京都市東山区縄手通三条下ル3弁財天町17
アートクラブビル4階
工事種別：内装のみ　新築
床面積：101m²(うち厨房17m²)
工期：1995年11月1日～12月10日
総工費：3200万円
＊営業内容
開店：1995年12月18日
営業時間：午後6時～午前2時
定休日：月曜　電話：(075)541-1199
経営者：真城成男
従業員：厨房2人　パート常時5人
合計7人
客席数：70席　客単価：3000円
主なメニューと単価：生ハム盛り合わせ1200　ペンネのゴルゴンゾーラチーズ1200　ミラノカツレツ900　エスプレッソ350　ワイン(グラス)500　(ボトル)2000
＊主な仕上げ材料
床：エポキシ樹脂系塗り床材特注色　モザイクタイル貼り10角
壁：寒冷紗パテシゴキの上骨材入り水溶性アクリル樹脂塗料
天井：寒冷紗パテシゴキの上AEP
照明器具：リネストラランプ150w　ミニクリプトン球40w
＊商店建築'96-03月号掲載

● ロータス (115P)
所在地：東京都渋谷区神宮前4-6-8
アイアムビル地下1階、1階
工事種別：内外装　全面改装
床面積：地下1階92.46m²(うち厨房12.17m²)　1階100.38m²(うち厨房29.63m²)　合計192.84m²
工期：1999年12月14日～2000年2月3日
＊営業内容
開店：2000年2月6日
営業時間：午前10時～午前4時
定休日：なし　電話：(03)5772-6077
経営者：(有)ヘッズ
従業員：サービス30人　厨房30人
合計60人(うちパート40人)
客席数：100席　客単価：2500円
客回転数：2回
主なメニューと単価：酸味のスープ350　バベットステーキ1000　コーヒー250　カプチーノ450　ビール500
＊主な仕上げ材料
床：塗り床仕上げ
壁：樹脂モルタル金ゴテAEPローラー塗装
天井：スケルトン　一部PB下地AEPローラー塗装
レジカウンター：アルミアイマイト仕上げ＋化粧板仕上げ
什器：ステンレスHL＋化粧板仕上げ
＊商店建築'00-06月号掲載

● シャルボン (118P)
所在地：大阪府大阪市西区北堀江1-6-23
工事種別：内外装　全面改装
床面積：1階180m²　2階63m²

データ内容は月刊商店建築掲載時のものです

合計243m²(うち厨房18m²)
工期：1999年11月10日〜12月2日
＊営業内容
開店：1999年12月9日
営業時間：午前11時30分〜午前0時
定休日：なし　電話：(06)4391-7215
経営者：(株)ブレインズ
従業員：サービス7人　厨房3人
合計10人(うちパート7人)
客席数：カフェ70席　バー30席
客単価：1600円　客回転数：2.5回
主なメニューと単価：コーヒー400〜　ケーキ450〜　パスタ800〜　カクテル・ダージリンクーラー600
＊主な仕上げ材料
屋根：スレート貼り
ファサード：モルタルOP塗装　一部杉材焼き板貼り染仕上げ
サイン：低電圧ネオン　書き文字OP塗装
床：エントランス／カラーモルタル金ゴテ押さえワックス仕上げ　カフェレストラン／モルタル金ゴテ押さえワックス仕上げ　カフェテラス／アピトン材染色ワックス仕上げ　パティスリー／ナラ材染色ワックス仕上げ　バー／樹脂タイル貼り
壁：PBt12.5二重貼りAEP塗装　一部モルタルAEP塗装
天井：エントランス／AEP塗装　カフェレストラン・カフェテラス・パティスリー・バー／既存木軸小屋組み補修OS
家具：テーブル／天板・アピトン材染色ワックス仕上げ　脚・スチール素地CL
什器：カウンター／天板・ステンレスHL　腰・白セメント金ゴテ押さえ
照明器具：スポット・ペンダント／スチールロッドベース布張り
＊商店建築'00-06月号掲載

● ニュートラル（121P）
所在地：大阪府大阪市北区曽根崎新地1-4-20　桜橋Mビル地下1階, 1階
工事種別：内外装　新築
床面積：地下1階206.64m²(うち厨房58.12m²)　1階87.35m²(うち厨房10.56m²)　合計293.99m²
工期：2000年11月5日〜12月5日
＊営業内容
開店：2000年12月9日
営業時間：月曜〜土曜／午後5時〜午前4時　日曜・祝日／〜午前0時
定休日：なし　電話：(06)4796-3300
経営者：(株)オックス
従業員：サービス10人　厨房8人
合計18人(うちパート12人)
客席数：132席　客単価：3000円
客回転数：1.5回
主なメニューと単価：スズキの紙包みオーブン焼き900　海老のアラビアータソース1200　ビール500　グラスワイン700　キールアンペリアル900　ジャマイカンコーヒー800
＊主な仕上げ材料
外壁：ケイカル板t8VP
サイン：カルブ材t10〜50切り文字EP
床：テーブル席／コンクリート床硬質塗り床材　ソファ席／パイン材t20フローリングOSワックス拭き

壁：地下1階／テーブル＆カウンター席・レンガタイル貼り　ソファ席・PBt12.5VP　一部アクリルミラー30角t2ランダム貼り　1階／PBt12.5VP
天井：地下1階／スケルトンVP　1階／PBt9.5VP
カウンター：ウオールナット材t50ワトコオイル塗り
＊商店建築'01-04月号掲載

● クィーンズコート（124P）
所在地：大阪府東大阪市吉田7-1-9　SEビル1階
工事種別：内装のみ　全面改装
床面積：52.3m²(うち厨房9.5m²)
工期：2000年6月1日〜7月11日
＊営業内容
開店：2000年8月4日
営業時間：午前7時〜午後8時
定休日：月曜　電話：(0729)60-0808
経営者：吉村吉雄　運営者：秦　比呂武
従業員：サービス3人　厨房1人
合計4人(うちパート3人)
客席数：34席　客単価：650〜700円
客回転数：2.5回
主なメニューと単価：クィーンズランチ950　和風カツランチ780　イタめし680　ボンゴレロッソ600　ブレンドコーヒー350
＊主な仕上げ材料
床：デッキ材フローリング貼り
幅木：デッキ材フローリング貼り
壁：PBt12.5AEP　一部タイル貼り　150角　R壁／リブパネルAEP　一部ステンレスHLフラットバー組み
天井：スケルトンAEP　一部米松単板練り付け染色CLパネル吊り
家具・什器：カウンター／米松単板練り付け染色CL　ソファ／ビニルレザー張り
照明器具：ステンレスHLプレート曲げ加工(一部スリット付き)
スクリーン：クリアミラー貼り
＊商店建築'01-01月号掲載

● ブレーク（126P）
所在地：愛知県碧南市松本町184　T-カッパビル2階
工事種別：内外装　新築
床面積：145.45m²
工期：2000年1月20日〜7月20日
総工費：7000万円(ビル建築費含む)
＊営業内容
開店：2000年8月4日
営業時間：午後5時〜午前1時
定休日：月曜　電話：(0566)46-6080
経営者：亀田幸孝
従業員：サービス7人　厨房3人
合計10人(うちアルバイト5人)
客席数：69席　客単価：2800円
客回転数：1〜1.5回
主なメニューと単価：スペアリブブレーク特製ソース980　スパゲティカルボナーラ680　大根とツナ和風サラダ580　コーヒー400　オリジナルカクテル500
＊主な仕上げ材料
床：ホモジニアスビニルタイル貼り
壁：レンガタイル貼り　クロス貼り　アルミ塗装複合材目地埋め込み　メラミン化粧板貼り

天井：PBt9.5クロス貼り　構造梁OP
家具・什器：ディスプレイ棚／メラミン化粧板格子組みアルミ塗装複合材埋め込み　スクリーンパーティション／スチールクロームメッキ格子組み　枠内クリアミラー貼りの上カッティングシートデザイン貼り
照明器具：円柱型特注照明／格子組みしぼり布貼り
＊商店建築'01-04月号掲載

● ヴィ　サ　ヴィ（128P）
所在地：大阪府大阪市北区大融寺町4-15　ホテルシーズ1階
工事種別：内外装　新築
床面積：157m²(うち厨房28m²)
工期：2000年5月25日〜7月15日
＊営業内容
開店：2000年7月19日
営業時間：午前7時30分(日曜・祝日は午前10時)〜午前1時
定休日：なし　電話：(06)6360-5813
経営者：中国土地(株)　A to Zディビジョン
従業員：サービス10人　厨房7人
合計17人(うちパート9人)
客席数：48席
客単価：昼700円　夜2500円
客回転数：3回
主なメニューと単価：モーニングセット380〜　ランチセット680〜　前菜500〜　パスタ800〜　コース料理3500・5000
＊主な仕上げ材料
床：タイル貼り　白041目地
壁：モルタルこすりの上プラスター金ゴテ押さえ
天井：PBt12.5AEPローラー塗装
家具：カウンター／天板・ブビンガ材ワトコオイル拭き取り　イス／ブナ材ウレタン塗装
照明器具：インゴマウラー(アルミパンチング板別注)　φ1.5ステンレスワイヤ張りに固定)
スクリーン：クリアミラー貼り
＊商店建築'00-11月号掲載

● パリヤ　北青山（130P）
所在地：東京都港区北青山3-12-4　MAKO北青山1階, 2階
工事種別：内装のみ　全面改装
床面積：1階163m²(うち厨房40m²)　2階110m²(うち厨房25m²)　合計273m²
工期：2000年11月12日〜12月27日
＊営業内容
開店：2001年1月18日
営業時間：午前11時30分〜午後11時
定休日：日曜・祝日
電話：(03)3486-1316
経営者：(株)巴里屋
従業員：サービス10人　厨房6人
合計16人(うちパート8人)
客席数：82席　客単価：4000円
客回転数：2.5回
主なメニューと単価：ほろ苦サラダ900　あみと納豆と塩昆布のチャーハン1000　えびしんじょのタイ風フリットトロピカルチリソース1200
＊主な仕上げ材料
外壁：ブロンズガラスt10L型アングル止め　アルミロールフォーミングルーバー
外部柱：H形鋼100×200鉄錆風エージング加工
床：モルタル金ゴテ仕上げ　一部シーラー塗装
壁：PBt12.5AEP　樹脂系複層仕上げ　タイル市松貼り55角　デリコーナー／銅板貼りt0.8飾りビス止め　バーコーナー／ガラスモザイク貼り
天井：PBt12.5AEP
家具：スチール鉄錆風仕上げ
＊商店建築'01-04月号掲載

● グリグリアバックスカフェ（132P）
所在地：東京都港区六本木5-1-3　ゴトウビルディング地下1階
工事種別：内装のみ　全面改装
床面積：レストラン247m²(うち厨房50m²)　アプローチ102m²　合計349m²
工期：1999年10月22日〜12月5日
＊営業内容
開店：1999年12月8日
営業時間：月曜〜木曜／午前11時30分〜午後11時(金曜／午前5時まで)　土曜／午後5時〜午前5時
定休日：日曜・祝日
電話：(03)5770-5335
経営者：(株)オートバックスレストランシステムズ
従業員：サービス12人　厨房8人
合計20人(うちパート13人)
客席数：レストラン／102席　カフェ／32席　合計134席
客単価：ランチ／約1000円　カフェ／600円　ディナー／3500円
客回転数：1回
主なメニューと単価：ランチ900〜　ディナーコース3000〜　ソフトドリンク400〜　ワイン／グラス500〜　デキャンタ1800〜　ボトル1900〜　ビール650〜
＊主な仕上げ材料
外部柱：ボンデ鋼板の上メラミン焼き付け
サイン：フレーム／ステンレスHL　アクリル内照式
床：タイル貼り300角　アルミチェッカードプレート貼り500角　テラコッタタイル貼り　イペ材フローリング貼り
壁：古レンガパターン貼り　ステンレスHL貼り　アルミ板貼り腐食仕上げ　銅板貼りサビ仕上げ　プラスター金ゴテ仕上げ　一部天然石貼り
天井：躯体表し　PBt12.5GP塗装　プラスター金ゴテ仕上げ
スクリーン：キャストアルミ
＊商店建築'00-05月号掲載

● バルコニー（134P）
所在地：東京都江東区有明3-1-22　TFTビル2階
工事種別：内装のみ　新築
床面積：83.74m²(うち厨房23.75m²)
工期：1996年2月26日〜3月17日
＊営業内容
開店：1996年4月1日
営業時間：午前11時〜午後9時
定休日：なし　電話：(03)5530-5625
経営者：(株)東京ヒューマニアエンタプライズ

データ内容は月刊商店建築掲載時のものです

従業員：厨房2人　サービス3人　合計5人
客席数：32席　客単価：900円
客回転数：6回
主なメニューと単価：ケーキセット750　コーヒー・紅茶・ハーブティー450　日替わりランチ1000　ディナーセット2300　ビール・グラスワイン500
＊主な仕上げ材料
床：メープル材フローリング貼り　トラバーチン貼り400角
幅木：トラバーチン貼り
壁：PBスタッコ風塗装
天井：PBt12VP　R天井部／スタッコ風塗装
家具：テーブル／桜材柾目CL　カウンター／桜材柾目CL　天板・大理石t30
＊商店建築'96-07月号掲載

● ちから（136P）
所在地：兵庫県神戸市兵庫区上沢通り1-3-2　湊川パークハウス1階
工事種別：内外装　新築
床面積：1階70.07m²（うち厨房16.5m²）　2階13.26m²　合計83.33m²
工期：1995年12月1日～1996年3月31日
＊営業内容
開店：1996年4月9日
営業時間：午前10時～午後8時
定休日：火曜　電話：(078)521-4044
経営者：(有)力餅　猪師一馬商店
従業員：厨房1人　パート2人　合計3人
客席数：カウンター9席　テーブル22席
客単価：550円　客回転数：2回
主なメニューと単価：手作りハンバーグ類850～900　シーフードドリア750　サンドイッチ各種600　コーヒー・紅茶350～　生ビール500
＊主な仕上げ材料
床：タイル貼り　一部カーペット敷き
壁・天井：PBt12複層仕上げ塗料塗り
テーブル：トップ／メラミン化粧板貼り
＊商店建築'96-07月号掲載

● イズントイットお初天神店（138P）
所在地：大阪府大阪市北区曽根崎2-5　お初天神ビル1階（現存せず）
工事種別：ファサードと内装　全面改装
床面積：155.14m²（うち厨房18m²）
工期：1996年6月13日～6月27日
＊営業内容
開店：1996年7月1日
営業時間：午前8時～深夜
定休日：なし　電話：(06)6366-5514
経営者：(株)セラリア
従業員：サービス3人　厨房4人　パート常時4人　合計11人
客席数：80席　客単価：1500円
客回転数：2回
主なメニューと単価：オールドリンク&フード各500（ごぼうサラダ　タコス　高菜とさしみの和風スパゲティー　地中海風サラダ　もちもちトマトグラタン）
＊主な仕上げ材料
ファサード：開口部／アルミカーテンシャッター　テント／キャンバス地テント貼り
サイン：既存スチール枠に乳半アクリル嵌め込み　FL内照式
床：大理石モザイク貼り　桜材フローリング　可動式フロア／桜材フローリング
壁：モルタル金ゴテ押さえパテ処理アクリル絵の具ペイントUC仕上げ
天井：PBt9アクリル系ペイント
カウンター部造作：天板／桜材　腰部／スプルス材一部パテ処理の上アンティーク風塗装
照明器具：天井埋め込み式照明オブジェ／鋼板t1.2クリア仕上げ　ブラケット照明／陶器製＋スチール丸棒曲げ加工および真鍮　可動式フロア取り付け照明オブジェ／スチール棒φ1.6曲げ加工の上FRP
＊商店建築'96-11月号掲載

● レゼ（140P）
所在地：大阪府和泉市小田町405-4
工事種別：一戸建て　新築
用途地域地区：第一種住居地域
建ぺい率：制限60%＞実効56.49%
容積率：制限200%＞実効147.58%
構造と規模：S造　地上3階建て
敷地面積：110.13m²
建築面積：62.21m²
床面積：1階62.21m²（うち厨房8.06m²）　2階52.78m²（うち厨房8.70m²）　3階47.54m²　合計162.53m²
工期：1995年12月14日～1996年5月21日
＊営業内容
開店：1996年5月26日
営業時間：午前11時～午前0時（金曜・土曜は午前2時まで）
定休日：月曜　電話（0725）46-0237
経営者：溝田はつみ
従業員：サービス2人　厨房2人　パート1人　合計5人
客席数：49席　客単価：2500円
客回転数：3回
主なメニューと単価：ベーコンとトマトのパスタ800　スモーク牛タン800　シフォンケーキ300　エスプレッソコーヒー300　カクテル700～　ワイン（ボトル）1300～
＊主な仕上げ材料
屋根：モルタル下地シート防水
外壁：サイディングボード貼り　一部ALC板VP塗装
外部床：カラーモルタルコテ押さえ　一部御影石乱貼り
〈1階〉
床：モルタル下地エポキシ樹脂系塗り床材
壁：PBt12.5AEP塗り分け　一部レンガタイル出目地　フロストガラスt8Fixの上ガラスナギット乱貼り　バックライト／ハロゲン球（35W）
天井：PBt9.5AEP塗り分け
カウンター：トップ／シオジ材板目単板貼りOSクリアウレタン塗装　腰部／カラーモルタルコテ押さえ
照明器具：円筒アクリルカッティングシート貼り装飾ガラス取り付け
〈2階〉
床：樹脂タイル貼り分け
壁：PBt12.5クロス貼り分け
天井：PBt9.5クロス貼り
＊商店建築'96-11月号掲載

● 屯風（142P）
所在地：京都府京都市左京区高野泉町6-11（現存せず）
工事種別：ファサードと内装　部分改装
床面積：39.04m²（うち厨房7.08m²）
工期：1996年9月1日～1997年3月10日
＊営業内容
開店：1997年3月12日
営業時間：午前9時～午後10時
定休日：なし　電話：(075)724-1001
経営者：稲本幸一
従業員：厨房1人　パート常時2人　合計3人
客席数：26席
主なメニューと単価：生ビール中ビン450　日本酒500～　トンカツ550　唐揚げ480　ごはんとみそ汁200
＊主な仕上げ材料
外装：松材板目板貼り　色モルタル　庇／松材葺き　開口部／蔵の内扉（アンティーク）
外部床：墨入りモルタル　白御影石
サイン：突き出し看板／鉄＋真鍮＋ネオン　看板／古屋の欅材看板（アンティーク）に真鍮文字取り付け
床：松材オイル拭き
幅木：松材オイル拭き
壁：松材および栗材化粧仕上げ　構造柱・梁／松材および杉材　土塗り壁サ・藁入り　一部真鍮製船窓取り付けケイカル板t6EP
天井：和紙貼りの上シナメイ（フィリピン産自然素材）重ね貼り　個室／竹組みの上麻貼り
家具：大テーブル&ベンチ／松材　カウンタートップ／楓材　個室テーブル／トップ・御影石　脚・スチール
照明器具：蚕棚アレンジ照明（竹＋シナメイ）　ステンドグラス＋鉄　和紙＋レーヨン糸　ラフィア（インドネシア産藁）＋和紙
＊商店建築'97-05月号掲載

● 資生堂パーラー（144P）
所在地：神奈川県横浜市西区高島2-18-1　横浜そごう2階
工事種別：ファサードと内装　全面改装
床面積：170.54m²（うち厨房47.73m²）
工期：1995年8月21日～9月19日
総工費：7620万円
＊営業内容
開店：1995年9月20日
営業時間：午前10時30分～午後7時30分
定休日：火曜　電話：(045)465-2373
経営者：(株)資生堂パーラー
従業員：サービス6人　厨房7人　パート・常時4人　合計17人
客席数：66席　客単価：1200円
客回転数：6.7回
主なメニューと単価：ランチ2000　ビーフカレー1500　チキンライス1300　オムライス1400　デザートセット1000　コーヒー450
＊主な仕上げ材料
外壁：アニグレ材単板練り付けサンディングシーラー処理の上ベージュ染色クリアウレタン5分ツヤ　スチールメラミン焼き付けt1.6　強化ガラスドアt12　クリアガラスt8Fix
床：カバ材フローリングナチュラルカラーUV塗装
壁：PBt12AEP　腰壁／アニグレ材単板練り付けサンディングシーラー処理の上ベージュ染色クリアウレタン5分ツヤ　スクリーン／フレーム・腰壁に同じ　メッシュ・籐材φ3ランダム張りクリアウレタン
天井：寒冷紗パテシゴキAEP
家具：特注／木下地ブナ材柾目突き板貼り染色ポリウレタン
什器：シナ合板エンジカラーウレタン　脚／スチールφ40クロムメッキ
＊商店建築'96-01月号掲載

● 束矢亭（146P）
所在地：東京都世田谷区玉川3-11-7　ティーズスクエア5階
工事種別：内装のみ　全面改装
床面積：209.51m²（うち厨房17.50m²）
工期：1998年4月21日～5月23日
＊営業内容
開店：1998年5月23日
営業時間：正午～午後11時
定休日：なし　電話：(03)5716-3383
経営者：ファブユニバーサル(株)，(株)ユナイテッドアローズ
従業員：サービス6人　厨房4人　合計10人
客席数：36席＋テラス26席　合計62席
客単価：4000円　客回転数：3回
主なメニューと単価：ランチ／1000（4種類）　730（子供のみ）　夜／野菜の入った豆腐餃子750　竹筒酒2合800　コーヒー500
＊主な仕上げ材料
床：ダグラスファー材フローリング木材保護塗装
壁：RC下地AEP　開口部／強化ガラスt5
天井：鉄骨組みテント地張り　一部和紙クロス貼り
家具・什器：ニヤトー材フラッシュ染色CL
植栽：大名竹　ナンテン
＊商店建築'99-01月号掲載